Leading Together

Leading Together

Mindfulness and the Gender Neutral Zone

NICOLE S. OLIVER SNYDER

Foreword by Soong-Chan Rah

WIPF & STOCK · Eugene, Oregon

LEADING TOGETHER
Mindfulness and the Gender Neutral Zone

Copyright © 2016 Nicole S. Oliver Snyder. All rights reserved. Except for brief quotations in critical publications or reviews, no part of this book may be reproduced in any manner without prior written permission from the publisher. Write: Permissions, Wipf and Stock Publishers, 199 W. 8th Ave., Suite 3, Eugene, OR 97401.

Wipf & Stock
An Imprint of Wipf and Stock Publishers
199 W. 8th Ave., Suite 3
Eugene, OR 97401

www.wipfandstock.com

PAPERBACK ISBN: 978-1-5326-0767-7
HARDCOVER ISBN: 978-1-5326-0769-1
EBOOK ISBN: 978-1-5326-0768-4

Manufactured in the U.S.A.   12/05/16

Unless otherwise indicated, Scripture quotations are taken from the New Revised Standard Version Bible, copyright 1989, Division of Christian Education of the National Council of the Churches of Christ in the United States of America. Used by permission. All rights reserved.

Scripture quotations from THE MESSAGE. Copyright © by Eugene H. Peterson 1993, 1994, 1995, 1996, 2000, 2001, 2002. Used by permission of NavPress. All rights reserved. Represented by Tyndale House Publishers, Inc.

To three Howards:
Howard E. Oliver (1941–1979), my heritage
Howard A. Snyder, my example
Howard J. Snyder, my partner in everything

my mother:
Suzanne J. Oliver, who believed in me most

and my children:
Samantha Nicole
Greer Olivia
Lysander Brian
Clark Howard JeeSung
who make me who I am
together, more like Christ

Contents

Foreword by Soong-Chan Rah | ix
Preface | xi
Acknowledgements | xiii

1 Introduction | 1
  The Rationale | 1
  The Problem | 7
  Hypothesis | 7
  Research Question | 8
  Biblical and Theological Foundation | 8
  Theoretical Foundations | 12
  Research Design | 15
  Intended Outcomes | 18
  Results | 19
  Summary | 19

2 Biblical and Theological Foundation | 21
  Hypothesis | 21
  Introduction | 22
  The Trinity, Whose Image Humankind Assume | 22
  Know God by Knowing Each Other | 33
  Know God by Knowing Another Culture | 44
  Conclusion | 58

3 Theoretical Grounding | 61
  The Problem | 61
  The Evolution of Social Roles | 61

    Mindfulness Research | 72
    Group Mindfulness: Discernment | 83
    Conclusion | 94

4 **Research Question and Design** | 96
    Hypothesis | 96
    Research Question | 97
    The Mindfulness Attention Skills Training and Group Discernment Practice Program | 97

5 **Results** | 109
    Quantitative Data | 109
    Qualitative Data | 116
    Significance of the Results | 118

6 **Summary** | 122
    What is Possible | 122

APPENDIX A | 131
APPENDIX B | 137

Bibliography | 141

Foreword

AT A CHURCH MEETING one evening, the senior pastor challenged the lay leadership team that the church did not exist for the needs of the individual congregants but for the sake of the glory of God's kingdom. One of the lay leaders took exception to this challenge and stated that if the church did not meet his individual needs, then there would be plenty of other churches that would meet his needs.

In a seminary classroom, a group of male students felt it appropriate to protest the gender of their instructor by turning their chairs towards the back when the professor entered the classroom. Her credentials as a scholar with multiple advanced degrees meant little to the students who revealed a complete lack of regard or humility towards an accomplished leader in the church.

A prominent church in the community emphasizes the need to honor their senior pastor. They elevate the leader to the point that any challenge to his hierarchical authority is considered a challenge to the Kingdom of God. A type of secular authority and leadership that doesn't even exist in secular society anymore replaces servant leadership.

During the years I served as a pastor of an urban church, one of the most significant challenges was spiritual development for congregational leaders. In complex settings where diversity and fluidity are given traits, congregational leadership takes on even greater significance. In my current calling as a teacher of future pastors, I continue to grapple with the significant challenge of teaching pastors how to engage in the spiritual development of congregational leaders.

Foreword

An added layer of complexity arises from the cultural and social imposition of historical and traditional gender roles that provide further alienation and disconnect for church leaders. The American church has come to rely upon stereotypes of effective leadership for Americans that reflect an unfettered machismo rather than authentic Biblical characteristics.

Nicole Snyder provides insight into a form of spiritual formation and leadership development that moves us beyond gender stereotypes. Emerging generations will resonate with the call for balanced leadership and balanced lives that move us beyond the drive and ambition of a previous generation's leadership dynamic. Beginning with a strong Biblical framework for mindfulness coupled with a deep theological analysis, Nicole Snyder presents leadership and ministry with new nuances and expressions. Her fresh perspective on leadership as mindfulness will challenge the church.

Well-researched and engaging multiple disciples, Nicole Snyder presents an ambitious and thoughtful work that confronts pre-existing dysfunction in the church context. As you read through this important work, allow Nicole Snyder to guide you through spiritual disciplines, formation and development that will serve the good work of God's kingdom in the local church.

Soong-Chan Rah
Milton B. Engebretson Professor of Church Growth and Evangelism
North Park Theological Seminary
Author of *Prophetic Lament* and *Return to Justice*

Preface

LAST NIGHT AS I was tucking my 11-year-old son in for the night, he said to me, "Mom, I wish that men listened to women better." So, bedtime was pushed back a bit while we had a conversation about stereotypes. Again. Despite the intentional effort to remove stereotypic language from our home, aside from the fact that every person in our family defies stereotypic sex-role categories (a father who values relationship over task completion; two older sisters who are strong, determined, and set on rigorous vocation trajectories; an older brother who is unearthly sensitive to his surroundings; and a mother whose roles were traditionally held by men) the generalization automatically fell out of his mouth. While my son's statement seems on the surface rather innocuous it belies the strength of that very human reflex to categorize people in order to rationalize. You see, before he made it to his bed he ignored my request that he stop watching YouTube videos on his phone, prompting a short lecture on the importance of his listening to me.

I am not sure where he heard the message that men generally don't listen to women. And, ordinarily he extolls the greatness of women—to which I first applaud and then remind him that one gender is equally equipped to accomplish a task as another. But it still astonishes me that stereotypic ideas and language pervade his thinking despite what he witnesses and hears in his own home. Such is the strength of the social system. A child's ideas are even more than ever out of a parent's grasp with the availability of every information source and social connection in the palm of the hand. It is for my son, for all my children, and for those who are exploited by a stereotype that I conducted the research that is now this volume.

Preface

This book is a slightly modified doctoral thesis. My quantitative research process and findings are included for those who welcome numbers and would like to see how I measured the effectiveness of mindfulness spiritual practice as a leadership style. The qualitative method I used is *especially* important because it analyzed the phenomenon, the nature of the system that underlies how we perceive good leadership. Things change only when we understand why things are as they are. Otherwise, we are doomed to plastering new programs (some, quite creative!) over older programs, while the institution remains static inevitably followed by entropy. The book's purpose, then, is to provide a comprehensive biblical and theological basis for a different way of leadership. It also provides a broad theoretical foundation that should be convincing if only by the overwhelming evidence for the benefits of mindfulness practice.

At the same time, while the language might be deliberate and precise, much of the text—particularly in chapters 2 and 3—is laid out in such a way as to orchestrate a movement meant to crescendo in fullness of understanding, a desire to make things right in the world. Chapter 5 provides results for pastors and spiritual leaders to consider. The conversation about a potential course action in chapter 6 is especially important.

The journey to this book's publication was long with many turns, roadblocks and construction, as well as a couple of highways and, perhaps a wormhole. The last might have been a dream. Or a vision of heaven? The journey included my own experience and my witnessing of friends, crushed, prevented to lead for what seems like inexplicable reasons, criticized for not leading according to an expectation that had little or nothing to do with actual effectiveness as a leader. Frustrating as it can be, the journey has not been embarked in isolation. We must be in right relationship with God to be in right relationship with others; and we must be in right relationship with one another to know and be in right relationship with God. This is righteousness and justice: to be in right relationship with God and one another whereby making things right in this world. I would love to see a larger dialogue around the issues brought to light. Please contact me if you would like to continue the exchange.

Acknowledgements

THE MOST INFLUENTIAL OF those who joined me on this journey are listed on the dedication page. In addition to these, my mother-in-law, Janice Snyder, who adjusted my focus to see the world with awe and wonder. My brothers—Gregg, David and Todd—and their families, each of whom hold very different views of their relationships with God and with the world. Yet, all of them have helped form a fuller understanding of God's image, and each of these beautiful people continue to love and support this work whether they agree or not. That is love.

Many others were crucial to this work making it to publication. Janet Campbell, the DMin Program Administrator at Denver Seminary from first contact to graduation with efficiency, expertise, and great compassion. The DMin Director upon my entering, Dr. David Osborn, saw me through a very difficult chapter in our lives; Dr. Timothy Dolan helped make it possible to complete the program. Dr. John Anderson, my advisor and first reader gave me the courage and an essential tool to finish it! Soong-Chan Rah, my second reader and whose work affirmed much of the culture-based aspect of the thesis. The Revs. Drs. Madelyn and Chuck Johnson who have always seen much more in me than I could see. Leza Shupe, most faithful friend and support. Elsie Demarest, who prayed me through; and Keith Meyer, who recognized my call when I began this ride.

There are countless others known and unknown to me, without whom this book could not have been written. Lisa Rieck who expertly edited the proposal. The pastors of Downers Grove First United Methodist Church, the Revs. Greta and Jim McDonald, who both opened the facility for the project to take place, *and* participated in the project. Jim Crandell who

Acknowledgements

generously edited the last sections of the thesis. Jennica, Kerri, Lenore, Carol, Kim, Eric, Alex, Linda, Annette, Kelly, Bill and Ann, and Ray and Ina who were faithful to the end. And, Cari Moore who steadfastly walked with us through the twist, turns, valleys and summits of the last five years of ministry. To all named here and known by God to move on my formation field: thank you.

1

Introduction

THE RATIONALE

PARKER PALMER SAYS IN his book *A Hidden Wholeness*, "Afraid that our inner light will be extinguished or our inner darkness exposed, we hide our true identities from each other. In the process, we become separated from our own souls. We end up living divided lives, so far removed from the truth we hold within that we cannot know the 'integrity that comes from being what you are.'"[1] Ministers and caregivers often feel that they are expected to be something they are not, which they rebel against. And, more often than not, they assert something else that is yet another division. The North American, pioneering, individualist imperative isolates the leader and forces each into a caricature of the self. "The truth is that the more dividedness we perceive in each other, the less safe and sane we feel."[2]

The human experience of wholeness is made possible by the very character of the Creator's expressed nature. That is, the God that created humankind is inclined toward and mindful of God's creation. (Ps 8:4–5) This God that Christians understand as Trinity is a relational God. The

---

1. Palmer, *A Hidden Wholeness*, 4.
2. Ibid., 16.

essence of the Trinity, then, is included in the DNA of humankind. Consequently, when creation is not behaving or operating as intended, something is restricted—divided—within the individual or community.

The current mobile technology-information reality the church occupies further exacerbates the isolated nature of the endeavor to be a community, and even just to *be*. Indeed, a recent study found that many people would rather shock themselves than spend time glancing inward.[3] Spiritual practices are clearly lacking, with centering prayer virtually unknown to ones so averse to being alone with their own thoughts. Mindfulness attention, a present-moment awareness that withholds reactionary judgment, is the underlying skill for these practices, and a great deal of attention in a variety of disciplines has been given to the myriad positive effects of employing this skill. Two of these are particularly salient to this work: (1) an increased ability to synchronize with others in a group setting and (2) expanded attention to otherness with a stance of openness and acceptance.

Without intentional pauses, it is easier to rely on external, superficial observations that separate one from another. One mode of separation that occurs between people is making and highlighting those differences to use as leverage for power or influence (vs. unity and cooperation). A specific focus for difference is sex (the biological characteristics male or female) or gender (the cultural roles ascribed to feminine or masculine). Conflicting messages are commonplace regarding what role women specifically play in leadership, and often create a bigger problem by ascribing a limited set of characteristics that define leadership to a woman's place therein. These will be discussed below, but the significant result is to perpetuate the isolated nature of leadership and the imperative to hold difference in position.

Defining Mindfulness

The concept of mindfulness is the subject of an abundance of books and articles on everything from self-help to addiction treatment. Leadership summits and managerial training all contain elements of one approach to mindful attention or another. Due to the volume of data that describes varying markers of "mindfulness," there is minimal consensus over a standard to measure traits and/or states of mindfulness. One key element for the purposes of this study is to understand mindfulness as distinct from

---

3. Wilson et al., "Just Think," 345.

self-esteem.[4] The goal of mindfulness practice is not to increase self-esteem, nor is such practice concerned with building self-esteem. Such focus too easily turns self-centered and is dubious as a motivator.

Most measures used to quantify elements that characterize mindfulness attention focus on self-report indicators of features and/or disposition of behavior in daily life. Characteristics of well-being, serenity, etc., are used to measure levels of perceived mindfulness. These are useful for understanding the traits that are involved in mindful attention, but they do not access the situational circumstances of awareness that occur throughout a given day. The various instruments that measure types of mindfulness practices show increased awareness in one sphere of focus, in working memory, and in short-term and long-term memory. For purposes of this discussion, the parameter of mindfulness is twofold: (1) intentionally paying attention with awareness of present-moment mental activity and (2) adopting an orientation toward the present-moment experience that is "characterized by curiosity, openness and acceptance" of circumstance and emotion.[5] Here, mindfulness will be defined as an awareness that arises out of the mode of being by paying kind attention, on purpose, in the current moment, without harsh judgment, to things as they are.[6] It is a present-moment disposition of curiosity and openness to the Spirit "bearing witness with our spirit that we are children of God" (Rom 8:16).

Efficacy of Mindfulness Attention

Measuring mindfulness for the purpose of research is anything but precise. Since each available instrument is designed to measure a specific type of attention and/or memory, it is difficult to compare consistency, validities, and reliabilities of assessments in multiple situations and types of study (e.g., current state versus pretest-posttest reliability). Still, a sufficient bulk of research across the spectrum of studies reports reliable statistically significant change as a result of implementing mindfulness practices—that is, sustained focused time that trains individuals to be more aware of internal and external realities.

---

4. Ryan and Brown, "Why We Don't Need Self-Esteem," 71–76.

5. Tanay and Bernstein, "State Mindfulness Scale (SMS)," *Psychological*, 1297.

6. Jon Kabat-Zinn developed the basic definition as a result of his research on pain management for cancer patients in the 1970s. Kabat-Zinn, *The Healing Power of Meditation*. See also Hart et al., "Mind the Gap in Mindfulness Research," 453–66.

For example, mindfulness training is shown to decrease anxiety.[7] Several studies demonstrate the effectiveness of mindfulness training to relieve symptoms of Post Traumatic Stress Disorder (PTSD). Specifically, attention and working memory (making creative connections) are dampened by stress and traumatic events.[8] Addressing such stress and anxiety is clearly beneficial to interpersonal relationships and to the community as a whole.

Many researchers who have studied the effects of mindfulness found that those who engage mindful practices regularly tend toward a simple lifestyle, including attention to environment care.[9] One such study focused on those who use scripture as a source for mindfulness practice.[10] A significant association was seen between higher engagement of such a practice and concern for often politically liberal interests such as social justice issues, environment care, equality of rights, openness to differences/cultures, etc.[11]

What is more, when research focus turned to group behavior, studies found that engaging in mindfulness practice enhanced social performance. That is, those who practiced mindful awareness in one study displayed greater inclination to cooperate and demonstrated evident synchronous group effort.[12] Other leadership training confirms that group mindfulness practice generates an increase in genuine group leadership.[13]

Parameters of Temperament and Leadership

Measuring personality traits and temperament is equally as elusive as mindfulness for precision quantification. Personality traits and social roles are largely influenced and shaped by the socio/cultural environment. Further, sociological study reveals that traits and roles shift and change across generations, as well as throughout the lifespan. Historically though,

---

7. Carmody et al., "An Empirical Study of the Mechanisms of Mindfulness," 65.

8. Aupperle et al., "Dorsolateral Prefrontal Cortex Activation," 69; and Carmody et al., "An Empirical Study of the Mechanisms," 5.

9. Brown and Ryan, "The Benefits of Being Present," 24; and Brown and Kasser, "Are Psychological and Ecological Well-Being Compatible?" 349–68.

10. Franzen, "Reading the Bible in America," 19.

11. Dy-Liacco et. al., "Spiritual Transcendence," 25; Lynch et al., "On Being Yourself in Different Cultures," 14.

12. Haas and Langer, "Mindful Attraction and Synchronization," 13.

13. Barton, *Pursuing God's Will Together*.

Introduction

characteristics of strong leadership are associated with stereotypical masculine attributes. And while feminist movements since the 1960s in North America have brought gender equality to the conversation, the result is effectually an invitation for women to display and enact these same stereotypical masculine characteristics. To the other extreme, it is asserted that a woman is necessary in leadership due to her uniquely stereotypic feminine traits, so that a balance therein can ensue.

The problem with both of these extreme views is that, now that a woman is afforded more opportunity to grow into her personhood and a man is increasingly challenged to expand his obligations, distinction between individuals is less dependent on stereotypic gender markers. That is, stereotypic traits historically demarcating sex have blurred, making necessary the conversation about what accurately characterizes good leadership, beyond the conventional gender role dichotomy.

What is more, well-accepted tools that gauge personality types and are often used to determine one's ability to lead, such as the Myers-Briggs Type Indicator, are based on a bifurcated scale that has been shown not to be valid from one circumstance to another (i.e., across time).[14] These tools are often used to serve as proof of gender difference across strengths and weaknesses. Yet, instruments that *are* psychometrically reliable and valid for measuring personality have shown that personality changes over the lifespan.[15] These changes are reflected in the responses classified by gender. In addition, developmental psychology has seen a shift in development as social structures have changed over time, adapting to the changing cultural context.[16] That is to say, the rules of behavior based on sex-type shift according to cultural changes and signal that, in fact, sex-role attributes are not based on biology but are culturally derived.

Copious neurological evidence documents the scant difference in brain activity in areas related to math and science among male and female children, particularly in subjects that in recent decades have downplayed significant gender differences, further reinforcing the assertion that much of the evidence for difference stereotypically ascribed to male and female is sociocultural.[17] While the specific nature and implications of the data

---

14. Boyle, "Myers-Briggs Type Indicator (MBTI)," 71–74.
15. Roberts and Mroczek, "Personality Trait Change in Adulthood," 5.
16. Greenfield, "Linking Social Change and Developmental Change," 18.
17. Eagly and Wood, "Sexual Selection," 276–77.no. 3–4 (2009 Also see Wood and Eagly, "A Cross-Cultural Analysis of the Behavior of Women and Men," 699–727.

now available are fascinating, it is beyond the scope of this project. Still, one element emerging from this line of inquiry is relevant here: the undue influence of sex-role stereotypes on leadership, and its impact on those who follow and learn. The number of church denominations that ordain women is increasing, making the question of expectations for leadership and how *good* leadership is defined all the more important. It is especially important because the resistance a clergywoman continues to sustain to her spiritual authority persists.[18]

A problem that immediately arises when research study is undertaken to explore the dynamics of leadership is that the research design itself limits the parameters of the inquiry. It begins with initial instruction for students of research design. Currently available research design textbooks that instruct students and researchers on dissertation and research development offer many suggestions for lines of inquiry and list commonly employed demarcations.[19] The most prevalent variable suggested is that of the *difference* between male and female responses to the research question. Immediately, the assumption is always that there will be a difference, and other confounding variables are overlooked.

This was the case in a 1989 study done by educational psychology researchers who approached the question of congruency between the respective gender of teacher and student and attendant biased attitudes toward learning.[20] The research set out to measure the effectiveness of teaching by looking at the sex of the teacher in relationship to the sex of the student, and to see if congruency between the sex of the teacher and student affected a student's attitude toward learning. The study found that such a congruency did no such thing. Instead, "we found only a main effect for sex role orientation with androgynous teachers (i.e., those who show warmth and concern plus are assertive and dominant), who produced the most positive student attitudes toward affective, cognitive, and behavioral intent learning. Students, whether male or female, were more affected by overall teacher qualities than by whether the teacher was male or female."[21]

---

18. See, for example, Imperatori-Lee, "Special Section," 89–107; and Hamman, "Resistance to Women in Ministry," 769–81.

19. Eagly and Wood, "Sexual Selection," 277.

20. Wheeless and Potorti, "Student Assessment of Teacher Masculinity and Femininity," 259–62.

21. Ibid., from the abstract.

Introduction

Students and those following the leadership of others, identify to a greater degree with leaders who employ a balanced leadership style. That is, displaying confidence *and* compassion, control *and* flexibility is more effective for a learning environment. Additionally, a broader range of leadership styles improves the ability to discern effective course trajectories. Removing stereotypic assignments to leadership traits will expand discernment and offer greater possibility for effective leadership.

My experience as a leader in six churches and three mission organizations was comprised of expectations that reflect stereotypic assumptions irrespective of my personal gifts and skill. When released to lead in spiritual development and biblical instruction, authentic relationships between the parishioners and myself, learning, and spiritual growth flourished. The newfound trust, however, threatened an already established hierarchy that valued control over growth, power in preference to organic community. This was true in my case as a clergywoman as well as for my youth pastor husband who champions relational ministry. Still, the double-edged assumption that a woman pastor *either* lead with power and self-possessed command *or* super-sensitive acquiescence was felt all too well. Noting that *effective* leadership seemed to be relationship driven with everyone's voice heard prompted my desire to investigate the veracity of this phenomenon.

THE PROBLEM

The specific problem addressed in this particular project was the pervasive imposition of stereotypic masculine characteristics expected of leaders that is neither effective nor an accurate understanding of good leadership.

HYPOTHESIS

The specific hypothesis generated to center the research was shaped in this way: As mindfulness attention and greater acceptance (openness) to members in leadership groups increase, members will identify to a greater degree with androgynous personality characteristics after a fourteen-week mindfulness attention skills training and group discernment practice program.

RESEARCH QUESTION

While other questions were also addressed, one question focused the research: Will implementing a seven-session program for mindfulness skills training and group discernment practice yield greater identification with more androgynous personality characteristics for individuals in leadership?

BIBLICAL AND THEOLOGICAL FOUNDATION

Image of God: Relational

It begins in the beginning. According to W. Sibley Towner, theological anthropology asserts: "a human being is defined by his or her relationship with God and God's other creatures."[22] By being made in God's image a person is characterized by something of God's nature, and that which God creates reveals something of God's character. A prominent feature is revealed by God's direct communication to the first people, Adam and Eve. Scripture is filled with examples, one after another, of God's initiating relationship with human beings. The first suggestion of the relationship-oriented character of God is in the use of the plural "let us make" in Genesis 1:26. God reveals a Divine relationship that is attentive to, and mindful of, the Other. And this Divine relationality exposes a shared responsibility between the members of the Trinity and between the Trinity and the image-bearers, a sense of equal power and intent.

Evidence for God's intention that those made in God's image—those who share in God's character—ought to relate with one another in the same way is made clear in the New Testament. God created humankind for relationship, that they be one as Jesus and the Father are one (John 17:11). The first passage most often evoked when equality is argued for is the Pauline phrase, "in Christ there is no male and female" (Gal 3:28). This passage is often said to refer to "*Haustafel* responsibilities," the New Testament household code that addresses relationships within the household, particularly between the husband and wife, father and child, and master and slave.[23] The crux of Paul's appeal to the Galatians, though, centers on love: "the only thing that counts is faith working through love" (Gal 5:6). And while Wayne Walden suggests that a lack of focus on roles in Galatians indicates

---

22. Towner, "Clones of God," 350.
23. Walden, "Galatians 3:28," 50.

INTRODUCTION

unconcern for its use, it seems that the relative absence emphasizes the truth that, *in Christ,* cultural expectations of the *Haustafel* and Pharisaic ritual hold no power over the identity of each (in community) in Christ. From the very start, God created humankind in God's image—male and female they were created (Gen 1:27). God told the first couple to fill the earth with their progeny and care for them. God exhorted the first of creation to steward the land, the animals and vegetation—together. No separate job descriptions are given—they are to share, to partner, in all things. Distinctions of role are made only after the Fall in the context of a curse. It is clearly not God's best, God's design, to separate people. This becomes even clearer when Jesus dwells with humankind much later. Yet, from the beginning, relationships have not been so united. After all, the curse in Genesis 3:16 speaks of a power struggle, not the mutual submission instructed in Ephesians 5:21.

One helpful approach to interpreting the creation narratives, and specifically the implications of humankind bearing God's image, is speech-act theory, which, in linguistics, indicates the basic unit of meaning in communicated language.[24] Performative speech allows for a perspective on the purpose of the creation narrative that does not focus on "created matter out of nothing, but rather the emergence of a stable community in benevolent and life-sustaining order."[25] Stephen Herring sees the proclamations and exhortations given to first humans as "revivification" of God, claiming humanity created in God's image is "the extension of the deity .... Humankind is the locus of divine presence and, as such, it should be highly cherished."[26] Indeed, Moshe Reiss, drawing from the Midrashim, posits, "God's truth is refracted in fragments of myth bound by the syntax of Scripture ... [and] to be human and to be God's image are not separable."[27] What most Bible commentators discern is the relational character of God: God in the performative, "let us"; God with humankind, "make in our image"; and, between humans, "it is not good for *ʾādām* to be alone." Just as there is no distinction among *Elohim*, so there is none among *ʾādām*; "both genders

---

24. As with any single approach to understanding Scripture, speech-act theory has some limitations. See Childs, "Speech-Act Theory," 375–92.
25. Herring, "A 'Transubstantiated' Humanity," 490.
26. Ibid., 494.
27. Reiss, "Adam," 182, 186.

exist in the *'ādām* from the outset . . . the human counterparts are fellowship and relationship . . . [not sexuality]."[28]

What is more, God created one from another to be *'ezer*, "a compositional phrase meaning 'matching him.'"[29] This counterpart, also created in the image of *Elohim*, is created to enact the possibility to *be* in God's image, that is, in relationship. "The phrase *'ezer kenegdo* (i.e., 'a helper corresponding to') occurs only two times in the Hebrew Bible and is a clear statement that in contrast to inferior animals (2:20), the woman is to be considered the spiritual and intellectual equal of man."[30]

The distinctions made during and following the sin act reflect the separation that came about between people who were created to be of one mind, that is, the mind of Christ. It follows, then, that personhood is not possible without another person. And, in this way, image and likeness tie together theology and anthropology.

Image of Christ: Community

The purpose of determining the nature of the relationship between the first two humans is not to determine that man and woman are equal. Exegetes can (and do) deftly show with great "clarity" that one is superior to the other. But that type of "reasoning is based upon a mentality of desire and struggle for power."[31] The example of the first church and its leadership—Paul, Silvanus, and Timothy, who intentionally eschew power to nurture young believers in Thessalonica (1 Thess 3:5–8)—renders such struggle irrelevant to the lived reality of Christ's body.

Indeed, much of the New Testament content regarding relationships is more focused on unity than on equality. Take Ephesians. The message of Ephesians is the importance of being of one mind—unity amid great separations. This unity has four dimensions: (1) unity between us and God (redemption and forgiveness allow us to be in God through and with Christ), (2) the cosmological union of heaven and earth, (3) the ecclesiological unity between Jew and Gentile, and (4) becoming a structure that is the temple.[32] The central instruction for how to attain such unity is via diverse

28. Towner, "Clones of God," 345.
29. Harris, "An Exposition," 40.
30. Ibid., 40–41.
31. Vogels, "It Is Not Good That the 'Mensch' Should Be Alone," 18.
32. Everding et al., "A Shaping Vision of Community," 426.

Introduction

gifts (Eph 4:1–6). This does not mean uniformity; rather, the same Spirit (in baptism, etc.) is the unifying principle, empowered by love. The core (head) is Christ who gathers all into and through himself (Eph 4:9, 10).[33]

Paul concludes his opening statement in chapter four with the phrase, "making every effort to maintain the unity of the Spirit in the bond of peace" (Eph 4:3). By separating from his Triune self, Jesus lives among humankind to bond and to be unified with us in identification with the life experience of humankind. The perfect unity with *Elohim* is temporarily suspended to (re)establish unity with the image bearers of God. The death, resurrection, and ascension make possible the resurrection and ascension of humanity into reunification with the Trinity. But this is only part of the deal. Unity with one another is a prerequisite. Indeed, maintaining "the unity of the Spirit in the bond of peace" (Eph 4:3) will usher in completion, maturity.

In Ephesians 4, Paul teaches that there are gifts of leadership, a balance of which is needed to perfect the church to do the work of God's kingdom. Lording any position over another, or holding one person in higher esteem than others, stunts growth. Rather, each is to honor the gifts in the other— none of which are attached to sex, race, or socioeconomic standing. Paul continues to instruct about not being "tossed to and fro . . . by every wind of doctrine" (Eph 4:14), as if we are children. It is not merely in the twenty-first century that questions of truth and divisions of churches dominate Christian conversation. Attention is given to the wrong thing. The current focus is to find distinctions in order to dominate the conversation (and one another)—to be "right" and to have "authority," as if the authority of the risen Lord were not enough. Rather, "every ligament" works—every cell, every bone, each molecule—to build the body "in love" (Eph 4:16). Disallowing someone to operate in the full giftedness of an image-bearer empowered by the Spirit of God is working against love.

The question is not one of gender or race or one particular categorization. The term *intersectionality* offers a useful construct for a less provocative and more productive—collaborative—conversation.[34] It moves away from the cultural directives that informed the New Testament writers and points to the truth that, in Christ, the endless cultural and historical situ-

---

33. For implications of dwelling on the image of the crucified Christ via the visions of Julian of Norwich that describe the work of Christ on the cross in great detail, see Bauerschmidt, *Julian of Norwich*.

34. Kartzow, "Asking the Other Question," 364–89. *Intersectionality* is an anthropological term that will be discussed in more detail in the "Theoretical Foundations" section below.

ations any community finds itself in make no difference to God when it comes to participating in the life and fullness of the body of Christ. That is not to say uniqueness is not important. To celebrate the particularity of individuals and cultures is to see and understand facets of God, but no single person or culture can contain all the facets of God in themselves, isolated from others. Rather, it is in the bond of peace, in love, "renewed in the spirit of your minds" (Eph 4:23), that a more complete (and completing) image of God is found.

Leadership functioning as a group with spiritual practices like mindfulness at the core will lead to a full, balanced leadership that reflects the true body of Christ. Spiritual practice and mindfulness attention is not an individual and isolated act (as some might suppose) when the mind is drawn to the center where Jesus resides. Richard Rohr explains: "Those who fall into the safety net of silence find that it is not at all a fall into individualism. True prayer or contemplation is instead a leap into commonality and community. You know that what you are experiencing is held by the whole and that you are not alone anymore. . . . [T]he mere reciting of prayers can also be, as St. John Cassian (360–435) called it, a *pax perniciosa*, or a 'dangerous peace.'"[35] It is dangerous to be so vulnerable as to defer to one another, especially as leaders. But it is still a measure of peace, and it is a bond—the bond of peace.

THEORETICAL FOUNDATIONS

Since humans are formed by countless factors, making observations on human behavior necessitates a multifaceted view. In this way, several theoretical perspectives work together to bolster the groundwork of this study.[36] The categories include the biological and behavioral sciences, as well as, anthropology and the domain of spiritual formation.

Anthropology, Sociology, and Neurobiology

According to the science of anthropology, social and cultural settings largely shape one's response to and identification with their sex role.[37] In an-

---

35. Rohr, "True Prayer Leads to Compassion," §1.
36. Cone and Foster, *Dissertations and Theses*, 119.
37. Donnan and Magowan, *The Anthropology of Sex*, 1–2.

Introduction

thropology, like in a growing number of disciplines (e.g., social, behavioral, and medical sciences), researchers are noticing the need for collaboration among the disciplines, and admitting that there are a number of factors that affect human behavior and development. Three emerging theories in the field of anthropology are: (1) multi-inheritance systems theory, (2) developmental systems theory, and (3) niche construction.[38] A new synthesis is now needed to understand inheritance, including three additional sources: epigenetic, behavioral, and symbolic. Symbolic inheritance occurs only in humans, and includes behavioral development, perceptions, and language/communication skills.[39] These will be developed further in chapter 3 below. What is important to note here is the emerging assumption that human evolution is "constantly constructing—and being constructed by—constituent elements of demography, physiology, reproduction, social interactions, cultural variations, complex information transfer, local ecological change and manipulation of the environment in intra- and intergroup contexts throughout the course of life history."[40]

The development of societies *in context* is the domain of Sociology. One subcategory of social interactions that is useful to consider is social identity theory, which asserts "that human beings categorize the world in order to bring meaning to their lives and especially to affirm the self's role in society. Group identity is constructed in the service of self-esteem. The theory suggests that there are three aspects of group formation: categorization, identification, and comparison."[41] All three of these features played a role in early Christian identity formation and the character ascribed to the ideal. For instance, attributes such as courage, strength, reason, and justice "defined ideal masculinity in the Roman world."[42]

Modern advances in technology reveal data in the field of neuroscience that also support such assumptions. Brain imaging (fMRI) studies show myriad ways culture influences the processing of relationships, the regulation of feelings and thoughts, and perception analysis.[43] For example, "Westerners tend to focus on objects (in an analytical, context-free manner), whereas East Asians tend to focus more on contexts, relationships,

---

38. Fuentes, "A New Synthesis," 13.
39. Ibid.
40. Ibid., 14.
41. Conway, "Dying to Be Men," 873.
42. Cobb, *Dying to Be Men*, 62.
43. Ames and Fiske, "Cultural Neuroscience," 72, 83.

and backgrounds."[44] Additionally, while gender identity has been broadly demarcated by social psychologists (i.e., masculine/feminine, as instrumentality/communality, respectively), neuroscience and cultural anthropology challenge this assumption. "Among other factors, identities are selectively activated by situational cues."[45] For example, in the educational system, stereotype priming plays a significant role. An observable gap emerged among elementary school children when they were primed to believe boys are better at math and science. The gap narrowed when they were told the reverse (i.e., told "girls are better").[46] Beliefs imposed and developed influence *brain structural* processes.

Medical scientists are not immune from influence, and are often predisposed to see sex differences when such differences cannot be explained by sex (that is, when a difference can only be evaluated when each subject is considered individually).[47] In one study, when a few endocrinologists suspended prejudice, they found that hormones associated with nurturing— oxytocin, most prominently—are produced in both sexes and fluctuate and surge during a child's birth.[48] This means that neurochemicals and hormones do not give support to there being a significant difference between the sexes as once assumed. Fulfilling (or not fulfilling) culturally ascribed sex roles is what influences hormone excretion levels.

Spiritual Discernment

Human personality and gender expression/role acceptance are incredibly complex systems. Culture, socioeconomic condition, time in history, biology, neurology, and even endocrinology all conspire to shape behavior. And while society and biology may appear to resolutely determine the trajectory of an individual's life expression, the mindfulness practice of discernment enables group members to consider an issue with improved clarity.

One of the most difficult barriers to development into fullness of personhood and "the full stature of Christ" (Eph. 4:13) is when religion is used to legitimize the power and dominance of one person over another.[49] Con-

44. Ibid., 83.
45. Echabe, "Role Identities Versus Social Identities," 30.
46. Neuburger et al., "A Threat in the Classroom," 61–69.
47. Jordan-Young and Rumiati, "Hardwired for Sexism?" 305–15.
48. Sanchez et al., "Oxytocin, Vasopressin, and Human Social Behavior," 319–39.
49. A Harvard study evaluated the Indian caste system using social dominance

trol based on power imbalance, or a religious system legitimizing such an imbalance that perpetuates leadership as a masculine-dominant domain, is not supported by a distinctly Christian theology of spiritual formation. Mindfulness practice in a leadership group invites reflection, attentiveness, and listening with imagination. When group members honor one another with intent while also attentive to the Spirit of God, finding common meaning and purpose is attainable. In doing so, leaders "promote the body's growth in building itself up in love" (Eph. 4:16). Sharing leadership with a unified effort makes love a more viable source for maturity, "the full stature of Christ" (Eph. 4:13).

RESEARCH DESIGN

Quantitative

Three inventories were used to quantify before and after program levels of mindfulness, sex-role type identification, and group cohesiveness. These are explained fully in chapter 4 and summarized here.

Mindfulness scales that measure the effectiveness of mindfulness techniques have shown increased health and the successful treatment of several addictions. Applying mindfulness techniques to a shared social setting is shown to benefit the health of a group tasked with leading collaboratively and to bring out characteristics that are attributed to stereotypical gender traits.[50] The Mindful Attention Awareness Scale (MAAS) is a 15-item inventory scored on a six-point Likert-type scale ("almost always" to "almost never"). The MAAS measures core characteristics of awareness and attention (e.g., "I find it difficult to stay focused on what's happening in the present," "I find myself listening with one ear, doing something else at the same time"). It also measures sensitivity to "awareness of what is occurring in the present." The MAAS has been used in research since 2003, and shows excellent psychometric properties, consistency, reliability, and validity across three distinct cultures, so it was chosen for this study.[51]

---

theory to show that karma is a "legitimizing ideology" that supports "antiegalitarian social policies and conventions": Cotterill et al., "Ideological Support for the Indian Caste System," 554–70.

50. Cone and Foster, *Dissertations and Theses*, 66.

51. Tanay and Bernstein, "State Mindfulness Scale (SMS)," 1288; Brown et al., "Out of the Armchair and into the Streets," 1041–46.

The Bem Sex Role Inventory (BSRI), developed by Sandra Lipsitz Bem in 1971, is a 60-item questionnaire using a seven-point Likert-type scale ("never or almost never true" to "almost always true") that measures stereotypically described femininity, masculinity, androgyny, and undifferentiated (e.g., "self-reliant," "analytical," "willing to take a stand"). The BSRI must be understood to measure how one fits into traditionally defined sex roles, and yet it illustrates that "labeling some phenomena as 'gendered' may be problematic."[52] At the same time, the BSRI remains a respected tool, valid and reliable to measure these same characteristics in relevant studies.

The Group Cohesiveness Scale (GCS) is a seven-item questionnaire using a five-point Likert-type scale ("strongly agree" to "strongly disagree").[53] The GCS was included to measure the degree to which individuals experienced cooperation in making leadership decisions.

Given limited access to sufficient populations to sample, three subsamples were selected and tested within the same timeframe.[54] These included ages ranging from nineteen to sixty-seven, spanning the array of socio-economic conditions and education. Participants were asked to join the study either directly by the researcher or by a secondary referral by others known to the researcher. The questionnaires were administered via Survey Monkey before the start of the intervention.[55] Each group participated in seven one-hour-per-week training sessions. The participants were instructed to engage in centering prayer through either the Centering Prayer App[56] or a hard copy trifold handout, and a phone text sent every two to three days that included a word picture and short centering prayer prompt. The prayer text was added to the program after the first session when several participants asked for some sort of reminder. A calendar was also given to each participant to help them keep track of the number of times they practiced personal meditation and the duration of each meditation session.

---

52. Parent and Smiler, "Metric Invariance of the Conformity to Masculine Norms Inventory-46," 327.

53. Wongpakaran et al., "The Group Cohesiveness Scale (GCS)," 58–64.

54. Davies, *Doing a Successful Research Project*, 55.

55. "Notably, multiple published studies have demonstrated no differences in the performance or psychometric properties of various psychological measures administered via paper-and-pencil and computer-based modalities (e.g., Gwaltney, Shields, and Shiffman, 2008)." Tanay and Bernstein, "State Mindfulness Scale (SMS): Development and Initial Validation."

56. Contemplative Outreach, "Centering Prayer Mobile App."

Introduction

It was not feasible to employ random sampling, so three groups from different locations (i.e., demographics) were used to expand the range of the population sampled and provide the possibility for comparison between groups.[57] Initially, a two-way dependent ANOVA was indicated as appropriate to determine the significance of the intervention.[58] The considerably fewer number of participants needed for the complex statistics and likelihood the Dependent Variable did not change as a result of the intervention suggested a paired samples t-test should be run on the BSRI pretest and posttest scores.

Qualitative

A compound phenomenon obliges a multifaceted research methodology. For this reason, I used a mixed-methods approach to better understand those complexities of processes and systems.[59] The project and research outlined in this paper are based on the supposition that once the impact of stereotyped expectations on leadership is known, *action will be taken to institute change*—in participants' expectations of leaders, and by using methods learned in the course to direct future leadership groups. Issues of power and social relationship also substantiate the importance of the study. As such, the research was based on a *transformative interpretive* framework. A phenomenological theoretical approach was used, as the research aimed to tease out the essence of the phenomena that influence expectations for leaders and the appropriateness of ascribed characteristics to what is considered "good leadership." Additionally, the research sought to bring "to the fore the experiences and perceptions of individuals from their own perspectives, and therefore [challenge] structural or normative assumptions."[60]

The research perspective was postmodern in its effort to seek answers from multiple perspectives (versus restricting individuals to categories), and the phenomenological approach was effective "at challenging structural or normative assumptions. [So] adding an interpretive dimension to phenomenological research, enabling it to be used as the basis for practical

---

57. Davies, *Doing a Successful Research Project*, 55.

58. Davies, *Doing a Successful Research Project*, 247.

59. Fetters et al., "Achieving Integration in Mixed Methods Designs-Principles and Practices," 2134–56.

60. Nesbitt, DMR-801 Research & Methodology Seminar.

theory, allows it to inform, support or challenge policy and action."[61] Focus group interviews were conducted in addition to the quantitative study outlined in the quantitative section above. Before and after the program, the researcher interviewed three of the leaders regarding their experiences and responses to components of the program, noting changes in perspective on leadership as a result of individual and group mindfulness practice.

The central question used was, What does it mean to be an effective (aka, "good") leader? Subquestions asked to clarify and elicit structural influences were included, for example, What does a person who exemplifies the term *effective leader* do? and, What is difficult or easy about being a good leader? An example of a procedural subquestion: What are the underlying themes and contexts that account for this view of effective leadership (e.g., stereotypic masculine-type characteristics)?

INTENDED OUTCOMES

Anxiety and depression pervade the North American population as a whole, and churches more specifically. Increasingly common to individuals in this stress- and anxiety-prone culture are symptoms of PTSD as a result of abuse; elevated blood pressure and heart disease related to immense burdens; and an over-reliance on technology to work more, achieve, and succeed.[62] Mindfulness practice for professionals and leaders who care for laypeople might facilitate effective healing, as those who suffer are more apt to receive and accept leaders who practice mindfulness more readily and with greater trust. Also, these skills can then be taught to victims to assist in more effective and lasting recovery.

To be sure, a community is inclined to follow the direction of its leaders. If individuals in a leadership group are empowered to notice the giftedness of individuals in the context of the community, and are each free to participate in leadership, the larger community is more likely see the impact and follow their example. The expectation for this project was that strengths and gifts, experience and education, and the unique character and the empowering of the Spirit of God as image-bearer would be considered and used in individuals irrespective of difference to a greater degree. The premise for executing this program was to demonstrate that practicing

---

61. Lester, "An Introduction to Phenomenological Research," §1.

62. See, for example, Broderick and Jennings, "Mindfulness for Adolescents," 111–26; Brewer et al., "Craving to Quit," 70–90.

mindfulness in a leadership group context would increase the likelihood that gender (or personality, race, etc.) would not be used to dominate or diminish another person or as an excuse to cower *or* unduly dignify.

RESULTS

Due to a number of unforeseen circumstances, of the approximately fifty people who originally indicated a willingness to participate in the research study, only twenty-three completed the course. And of those remaining, twenty actually participated in some or all of the sessions. The complex statistical analysis needs to process a far greater data set. A simpler statistic was recommended to analyze the tests individually. The results of these are discussed in chapter 5.

Since the initial analysis could not be performed, the intervention could not be proved to effect the level of one's identification with stereotypic sex roles with statistical significance. The results from the pretest and posttest *focus group interviews*, however, *did* indicate a possibility that such change occurred. A discussion of these results is also included in chapter 5 below.

The focus group that was interviewed before and after the project comprised three project participants. The pre-project focus group described leaders who tend to occupy leadership positions with words that indicate an aggressive posture, as operating like a business, and competitive solo leaders as the norm for "successful" churches. In contrast, the post-project focus group interview immediately focused on good leadership as collaborative. Interviewees used words that described collaboration with significantly greater frequency than in the pretest interview. And when questioned concerning structural (cultural/anthropological) meanings that inform underlying themes and contexts, the focus group members seemed to have a better grasp of what the question was asking. Implications of these qualitative data are discussed further in chapter 5.

SUMMARY

Implications of the research are examined more closely in chapter 6. The data gathered from the MAST-GDP project and supporting research revealed the impact mindfulness spiritual practices in a group setting have on pulling down self-erected walls and opening one's eyes to see clearly into an *other*. The data also highlighted the enormity of the need and of the task presented the church. If it is true that mindfulness attention practices can have a significant effect on so many aspects of life (lowered blood pressure and heart rate, decreased anxiety, greater cooperation among group members, etc.), it seems intuitive that intentionally engaging in and teaching these practices in the church are wise and necessary.

Chapter 6 includes a discussion of the scope of the task the church has to tackle especially the pervasive use of handheld computers that invite impulsivity, effectually rendering reasoned reflection unavailable to the habitual user. The results of the research study hint at the generalizing applicability of this kind of program to address the issues of attention and focus. The changing nature of leadership, and shifts in society in general are noted, along with recommendations for further research to answer these changes.

A major shift in how emerging generations respond to leadership is discussed, as well, in the last chapter. The challenges to deal with what new technology can bring to, and how it can thwart community, are outlined. How these can be investigated further is also discussed. A general lack of commitment is characteristic of emerging generations and an obligation to its leaders is similarly lost. Some suggestions are proposed for the church to consider that might influence the community in light of, and with the use of, the technology that plays a role in the development of young people in the twenty-first century. Finally, the project did result in a general understanding that theory has seen a spark of motivation to action by the participants to produce healthy people who work together and promote the health and maturity of the whole, while moving in the strength of personal unity with the Triune God—collectively.

2

Biblical and Theological Foundation

"To the mind that is still, the whole universe surrenders."
                                                    Lao Tzu[1]

"What are human beings that you are mindful of them,
mortals that you care for them?
    Yet you have made them a little lower than God,
and crowned them with glory and honor."
                                              (Ps 8:4–5)

HYPOTHESIS

How does scripture and theological tradition inform the supposition of this study? As a reminder the hypothesis is: As mindfulness attention and greater acceptance (openness) to others increase, members will identify to a greater degree with androgynous personality characteristics after mindfulness attention skills training and group discernment practice.

---

1. Lao-Tzu, "The Tao-Te Ching," 1891.

INTRODUCTION

The author of the eighth Psalm reveals that God is mindful of humankind. This God speaks directly to humankind and imparts glory as the created glorifies God. Yet the creation narratives in Genesis 2 and 3 describe the process of relational disconnect when the first humans turn a deaf ear and are not mindful of God's presence and promise. Genesis 1:26–28 asserts that humankind was made in God's image and that God spoke to them, establishing personal relationship. Genesis 2 continues the storyline, describing Eve and then Adam consulting only the self, and making choices not aligned with God's instruction and promise. By not being mindful of the covenant God instituted, unity is dissolved and the unique character of the individual (created in the image of God) becomes emphasized and perverted.

This chapter will describe how God who is revealed as Trinity is, in essence, relational. The personal character of the Trinity obliges each Person of the Trinity to remain mindful of the Other. That humankind is made in the image of the Trinity discloses a crucial aspect of what it means to be human: to be mindful of God, and to be mindful of one another. For the purpose of this treatment, mindfulness is defined as an awareness that arises out of the mode of being by paying kind attention, on purpose, in the current moment, without harsh judgment, to things as they are.[2] It is a present-moment disposition of curiosity and openness to the Spirit "bearing witness with our spirit that we are children of God" (Rom 8:16).

THE TRINITY, WHOSE IMAGE HUMANKIND ASSUME

A systematic treatment of the doctrine of the Trinity is well beyond the scope of this book. For this reason, the argument will approach the doctrine of the Trinity from a strictly theological posture based on the prolific discussion already established. And because the Christian church has historically gathered around principles concerned more with "correct" *thinking* than with the *relationship* implied in Christian teaching on the Trinity, the

---

2. Jon Kabat-Zinn developed the basic definition as a result of his research on pain management for cancer patients in the 1970s. Kabat-Zinn, "Mindfulness-Based Interventions in Medicine and Psychiatry," 93–119. See also Hart et al., "Mind the Gap in Mindfulness Research," 453–66. These principles also found in scripture: Phil 4:8; Col 3:2; Prov 3:5–6; Matt 6:34; Rom 12:2; 1 Cor 13:4, Ps 23, 1 Kings 19:12, Ps. 46:1–7, 10a, etc.

discussion will develop from the premise that the Trinity itself is revealed as relational.³ Trinitarian theology, according to Jürgen Moltmann, "starts from the interpersonal and communicative event of the acting persons about whom the biblical history of God tells."⁴ Mindful attention to the other makes possible the interpersonal and communicative event that occurs in the Trinity.

The Trinity as Mindful of the Other

A Greek term often used to describe the Trinity is *perichoresis*, "triadic intersubjectivity," or the interrelationship between and among the three Persons that constitute the Trinity. The correlative Latin words also used are *circumincessio* and *circuminsessio*, movement *and* rest. Each member of the Trinity is "at once persons and spaces for movement," giving up space to the Other to make space only to be filled up, and they exist as more than individuals by being mindful of (and formed/informed by) the Other.⁵ The movement is a dwelling indwelling, perpetually aware of each Other, in each moment.

In the Jewish tradition, the noun *shekinah* is the place or space where God's presence dwells, fills. Jürgen Moltmann posits that the Sabbath, as in the *Shekinah*, is instituted for this purpose—for the indwelling of humankind—and is like a hurricane: the Persons of the Trinity "are *at once persons and the spaces for movement*."⁶ The Scripture reveals this process in the experience of Jesus, who experiences the grief and sin of humanity; the experience of the Father whose Son cries out, "Abba" (Love); and the experience of the Spirit in fellowship, present with God and with humanity.⁷ It is grace, love, and fellowship.⁸ Herein lies another clue to what it means to image God: indwelling.

---

3. This is most clearly articulated in Grenz, *The Social God and the Relational Self*. See also LaCugna, *God for Us*; Peters, *God as Trinity*; Zizioulas, *Being as Communion*. For relationship as *attributional*, see Gunton, *Act & Being*.

4. Moltmann, *Sun of Righteousness, Arise!*, 149. For an exposition on Genesis 1 and the God who "acts by speaking," see Auld, "Imago Dei in Genesis," 259–62.

5. Ibid., 154.

6. Ibid., 155, emphasis mine.

7. Ibid., 159–160.

8. Grenz, *The Social God and the Relational Self*, 43.

The Old Testament comprises story after story of God's desire and attempts to dwell among the people of Israel. It is expressed by the word "to dwell," שָׁכַנְתִּי *shakhanti* [BHS-W4] as a verb—active, intentional, communicative (Exod 25:8; 29:45; 1 Kings 6:13; Jer 7:7; Ezek 43:9; Zech 2:10, 11; 8:3). So, as *perichoresis*, the Trinity is revealed as active and intentional, Persons who dwell and indwell, who act as individuals while making room for the Other, moving *and* making room for rest. Thus, to image this God that indwells with mindful attention to the Other within the Trinitarian Self is to dwell with each other with mindfulness of one another by making space. It is a movement, a dance that gives up one's place so that another may fill it and then to become more like oneself—and, more like the image of the Creator.

Trinity as Imaged and Likened

Who is it that humankind images? What are the identifying features that are God and that describe what it is to be truly human? When God creates the first human, God speaks in the plural: "let us make" (Gen 1:26). Indeed, the name of God used by the author of the first creation narrative, *ʾelōhîm*, is in plural form, establishing relationship as God's very mode of being.

First, matters of grammar and language give some clues to what the priestly writer is communicating about God. Noted above, the plurality of the name *ʾelōhîm* indicates one God while many. To further emphasize the point, the opening phrase "let us make" [נַעֲשֶׂה] (Gen 1:26) leaves little doubt that plurality is characteristic of *ʾelōhîm*. The pronoun "our" in "in our image, according to our likeness" [בְּצַלְמֵנוּ כִּדְמוּתֵנוּ] (Gen 1:26) seals the deal. What is interesting is that the first part of this phrase, "our image," is a masculine construct, while "likeness" is in the feminine construction.[9] Then, throughout the two verses (vv. 26–27), both singular and plural pronouns are used interchangeably. So in verse 26, there is the emphatic "like our likeness" (*kidmûtēnû*, "as," or "like" "our likeness"), but then "image" [צֶלֶם, *ṣelem*] alternates: in verse 26, *bᵉṣalmēnû* (plural, "in our image"]; then, in verse 27, *ʾelōhîm*, created "in his own image" [בְּצַלְמוֹ] *bᵉṣalmô* (singular, "in his image") ... "in the image of God" [בְּצֶלֶם אֱלֹהִים] *bᵉṣelem ʾelōhîm*, singular image to the plural subject "them."

---

9. More on the significance, or insignificance, of gendered language pertaining to God is discussed in a later section.

Biblical and Theological Foundation

Image (ṣelem) and likeness (dĕmût) are used together in parallel in only two passages in the Old Testament: Genesis 1:26 and 5:3. An initial question is raised concerning the interpretation of the preposition, bet, in the Hebrew construction בְּצַלְמוֹ, which translates "*in* our image" or "*as* our image." The traditional, Platonic view (also contained in the Vulgate) takes the first meaning, whereas current interpretive work has increasingly shifted to the latter. The first carries the implication of copy, while the second translates as "statue." In its ancient context, the implication is that the statue carries and embodies the power of the ruler in whose image it was made,[10] more than merely representing the authority of the ruler.

A second issue at play in understanding what it means to image God pertains to two general themes. One suggests that image and likeness indicate the *substance* of that which is being imaged and its likeness. This line of inquiry is concerned with issues of "essence" and matter. Questions of substance elicit answers of fact and doctrine. The other broad category sees image as found in "relationship"; that is, as Karl Barth advanced, the disposition or inclination to relate with God and each other *is* the revelation of God's image in humankind.[11] Towner points out that Genesis 1:26-27 "and its echoes in 5:1-2 and 9:6 point human relationships in three directions": The divine image is revealed in worship and covenant with God, in relationship (oftentimes sexually) with one another, and as stewards of the earth.[12] All three of these aspects of relationship oblige one to abide a posture of mindfulness. That is, one must be attentive (i.e., pay attention) to God in worship, intentionally being present to God's presence in that moment, with an openness to hear, or notice, God's presence, without harsh judgment, as one is in that moment. This posture also has bearing on relating to one another in intimacy and to understanding and caring for the earth, for its flourishing.

Towner's assessment is, "All biblical theology turns out to be theological anthropology, which means that a human being *is defined by* his or her relationship with God and God's other creatures."[13] At the same time, pru-

---

10. Welz, "Imago Dei," 74–91. The parameters of ṣelem in the CDCH are: (1) image, replica, to avert divine wrath (1 Sam 6:5); image of deity (Num 33:52); sexual image of human male or male deity, or phallus (Ezek 16:17); erotic painted engraving (Ezek 23:14); (2) image, likeness of God (Gen 1:27); human father (Gen 5:3); (3) transitory image, silhouette, semblance (Ps 73:20).
11. Towner, "Clones of God," 349.
12. Ibid.
13. Ibid., 350.

dence cautions against thinking that "the task of theological anthropology is one of definition."[14] Anthropology asks the question "what is humanity?" in order to query theologically the image in which humanity was created; the inclination is to *begin* with human characteristics and the static place and time in which humankind exist. And while it is important (necessary) to read the Genesis narrative through a soteriological, Christological lens, to do so exclusively risks reducing the image of God to "essentialist concepts" (e.g., substance).[15] The result of such a reading has opened up the discussion of humanity's role in issues of justice and in making things right in the world, but an overemphasis makes the lens vulnerable to secularization and can diminish the divine that characterizes that image. A threefold mindful attentiveness to God in worship, to one another in intimacy, and to the earth for its flourishing provides a corrective.

God Is Mindful of Humankind

The eighth psalm is a summary of God's relationship to creation, salvation, and eschatology. It describes "human dignity" and the conferred vocation of "dominion" that reflects God's rule, that is, "God's Kingdom of justice and peace, in which the whole of reality enjoys fulfillment together with God."[16] Still, the relationship entails more than knowing and being aware of God's name; dignity and vocation involve experiencing the reality of God's relating. How humanity acts—exercising dominion, covenanting with one another—images God by its *orientation*. God is oriented toward—mindful of—humankind.

By looking to the liturgical Psalm 8, Alistair McFadyen promotes a "theological deracination," a tearing up by the roots, that places the theological anthropology emphasis on the divinity: the image *of God*.[17] According to McFadyen, by making Genesis 1–3 the starting point for understanding God's relationship to humankind, a static rendering of God's image is nearly unavoidable. At the same time, Scripture does not contain any explicit anthropological markers of God, clearly on purpose: "humanity is neither the center nor the primary focus of scripture; therefore, interest in

---

14. McFadyen, "Imaging God," 919.
15. Ibid., 920.
16. Ibid., 925.
17. Ibid., 922.

the human as a theme is derivative and secondary."[18] The climax occurs in the fourth verse, "When I look at your heavens, the work of your fingers, / the moon and the stars that you have established; / what are human beings that you are mindful of them, / mortals that you care for them?" (Ps 8:3–4). McFadyen continues,

> Psalm 8 has a shorthand code whereby it rolls up the whole history and future directedness of God's relating in its orientation toward human well-being, flourishing, and consummation: *God's mindfulness* (v. 4). And it is in the context of wondering acknowledgment of the status that affords human beings that it articulates the anthropological question in a specifically and definite theological register.[19]

Herein lies the crux of the matter: "the *mindfulness of God* represents the point of departure, the *telos* of the question [of God's image] and not merely an after thought tacked on to the end of a thought already in independent movement."[20] The anthropological question is raised in the context of God's relationship with humankind. This God is mindful. And this God is mindful of all of humankind. In other words, "Psalm 8's way of asking the anthropological question presupposes an answer to the *theological* question: Who is God?"[21]

As a psalm, the song begins with an invocation of God. But, even more significant, the invocation calls God by name: "O Lord, our Sovereign, / how majestic is your name in all the earth!" (Ps 8:1). The profound suggestion is that the God being addressed is relational, one who is named and will answer. What is more, the name itself is praised. It is called holy because the name is a self-revelation, that is, not given by humans but revealed via God's directly relating to humankind:

> The giving of the Name represents also the self-identification of God as the Holy and transcendent Lord who determines to be God by being *for* human beings, and *for* us in such a way that makes Godself available for, while seeking and eliciting imaging human response. Second, use of the Name recalls the event in which the Name was given—at once seen both as pivotal in and

---

18. Ibid., 923.
19. Ibid., emphasis mine.
20. Ibid., 924, emphasis mine.
21. Ibid.

representative of the whole history of "mindfulness" between Yahweh and His people.²²

What is revealed about God's giving of the name and the human response of praise, again, has more to do with how God uses that response. It is more than knowing and being aware of God's name; it is experiencing the reality of God's relating. How humanity acts—exercising dominion, covenanting with one another—images God by its *orientation*. All that is given humankind to do is given by "divine grace," and it is fully used and effective when it is oriented in praise to the Giver. Praise turned inward distorts and brings chaos; ". . . human power [is] shaped and qualified by doxology."²³ So to participate in God's glory—in praise—is to participate in the life-giving, creative power of God and in being God's image. This means, then, that the anthropological question is not so much "what is humanity?" Rather, it is "what does it mean 'to be a worshiping human, or one who praises, laments, longs, hopes, prays, complains, or trusts the God of Israel?'"²⁴ It reveals the place of the human in the whole narrative, which is to live the life to which God calls us: *Be* righteous, just, loving, merciful.

McFadyen calls the eighth psalm "a liturgical performance."²⁵ When asking the question "what is humanity?" the answer is in the performance of the hymn, in the act of praise—not in facts; the answer is contained in the act. "This seeking of the human, rather than description, is . . . the chief anthropological interest of Christian faith and theology."²⁶ Claudia Welz comes to a similar conclusion: "The [biblical] text does not make it explicit what the *imago Dei* consists in, but it explicates *to what end* the human being is created as God's image."²⁷ The idea, initiated by Augustine and redefined by Dietrich Bonheoffer, is that the human end is freedom. But this freedom is not a "quality of the human being, but rather a relation, since freedom is not something that the human being has for him- or herself, but *for* someone else."²⁸ To be human is to be mindful of, giving space to, another.

22. Ibid., 927.
23. Brueggemann, *The Message of the Psalms*, 38.
24. Briggs, "Humans in the Image of God," 122.
25. McFadyen, "Imaging God," 931.
26. Ibid.
27. Welz, "Imago Dei: References to the Invisible," 78, emphasis mine. Echoed in LaCugna, *God for Us*, and the Cappadocian Fathers.
28. Welz, "Imago Dei: References to the Invisible," 80, emphasis mine.

Biblical and Theological Foundation

Mindfulness with Meaning: Relationship

Mindfulness practices are not a new phenomenon. Buddhism, based on the teachings of the circa fifth-century BCE sage Gautama Buddha, introduced a system of meditative practices to reduce the impact of suffering.[29] In general, these practices correspond to Jewish beliefs. Principles of liberation and community, simplicity and pure thinking, are congruent with the precepts given to the ancient Israelites. A significant difference between the two, however, surrounds the prominent feature of karma in Buddhism (destiny or fate, a death and rebirth that follows from the effects of past deeds) and grace in Judaism. The Irish rock band U2 rightly describes grace in the song entitled "Grace" as traveling *outside* karma.[30] The difference lies in the focal point. Buddhism assumes no deity, positing that everything can be in harmony if only one focuses enough, detaches from the pain enough, tries hard enough. The Trinitarian God *is* the focal point—within the Trinity and between God and humankind. The difference is the reality of relationship.

Following the death and resurrection of Jesus, the developing church began the work of living out this new reality of freedom—freedom to relate to a holy God and the power to do the same with each other. But it seemed necessary to make clear theologically what it means for such a God to be Creator *and* Father *and* live among us. Irenaeus, a second-century bishop, formally advanced the Latin term for "Trinity" to describe God—one God (nature), three distributed, "administered," or "economized" by Son and Spirit.[31] Yet it was the fourth-century Cappadocian theologians, Saint Basil, Gregory of Nyssa, and Gregory of Nazianzus, who brought significant contributions to the development of the doctrine of the Trinity. The crux of their argument is that the Trinitarian God is understood as "Divine Relations." To participate in the work of theology, however, it is not enough to outline ideas and definitions for characteristics of God. It is not enough to be attentive to the syntax of language or the historical context of Scripture. Theology is possible only when approached with contemplative—mindful—engagement with God.

---

29. For Buddhist application to mindfulness practices see Kabat-Zinn; Ozawa-DeSilva and Ozawa-DeSilva, "Secularizing Religious Practices," 147–61. And, in comparison to Trinitarian theology, Phan, *The Cambridge Companion to the Trinity*.

30. U2, "Grace."

31. LaCugna, *God for Us*, 28.

For Gregory of Nazianzus and Basil, "theological speculation is contemplation (*theōria*), the unitive vision that follows upon illumination." Theology is possible only with reflective attention toward, and engagement with, God. Again, for Gregory and Basil, "At most the theologian can say that God is *for us;* to speak about the mystery of God (*theologia*) is possible only because that mystery is recapitulated in the economy of salvation (*oikonomia*)."[32] In other words, a description is only possible by participating in the relationship made possible by the redemptive work of Christ. And even then, in Catherine Mowry LaCugna's view, the economy discloses *how* God is, not *what* God is.

What made discussion about, and understanding of, the nature of the Trinity difficult surrounded the issue of language across continents. For Gregory, the essence of God is untouched by the question of whether God is, for instance, begotten or unbegotten. "Inquiring into the essence of God will leave unaffected the personal property or differentiating characteristics (*idiotēs*) of being begotten or being unbegotten."[33] But this is precisely where consensus becomes so difficult: The terms *hypostasis* and *ousia* were basically interchangeable until distinctions between them were demarcated at the end of the fourth century. Athanasius used them interchangeably when he defined *hypostasis* as a "metaphysical term for an independent object" but then described *prosōpon* as non-metaphysical for the individual members. In fact, until 369 BCE, no reference was made to three persons and one *ousia*.[34]

What is more, *hypostasis* was used in different ways—transitive *and* intransitive— depending on the locale. So, for example, humanity might be referenced by *ousia*, the common nature of humans. Paul and Timothy are two *hypostases* of shared *ousia*. But the distinction between Father and Son is described in reference to their circumstances of being, respectively, unbegotten and begotten (*agennētos* and *gennētos*)—or their "relations of origin."[35] So the Cappadocians further delineated modes of being. Essentially, according to LaCugna, the three hypostases is God's way of being known to us, when the essence of God is unknowable, while both are "inexpressible."[36] To know God *is to be in* relationship with God.

32. Ibid., 56.
33. Ibid., 64.
34. Ibid., 66.
35. Ibid., 67.
36. Ibid., 68.

Biblical and Theological Foundation

Mindful of Each Other: Image Bearers

God reveals who God is through relationship. What does it mean to image this God? In a recent collaboration between semiotics and visual studies, a new field of image theory, designated *Bildwissenschaft*, is developing. This new perspective brings attention to the way an image (e.g., painting, sculpture) is perceived. The image signifies by pointing rather than being described, a gesture that "moves the viewer to turn around."[37] It points past the self to the other and communicates beyond the image, revealing something of the creator, in much the same way a parent holds a child's hand while pointing with curiosity to something else.[38] By knowing another individual, the unique aspect that images God in that person is laid bare. Yet in order to know another, one must be mindful of, attentive to, that person, to discover where the focal point might lay.

Building on the conclusion of LaCugna and the Cappadocians that the act and relation of the Trinity reveals a "God *for* us," McFadyen further suggests that the self-revelation of God who *speaks* the name directly to humankind discloses a God who is for us and is mindful of us. With that view in mind it is possible to see God's action in the creation narrative in a new light. God creates with speech and blesses the creatures in Genesis 1:22, and again with the creation of *hā'ādām* in 1:28. The difference is that, in this last instance, it is a direct address, לָהֶם ("said [to them]"), and reveals God's initiation of relationship. The phrase "and God said" is used nine times in Genesis, but only once is it "and God said *to* [someone]," in verse 1:28.[39] Gerhard Ebeling describes this as the *Wortgeschehen*, "the *event of the word* which can happen only between God and man and between human beings."[40] It is an event of speech that creates the person—created in the image of the Speaker. Which means it is well beyond the denotation of image as representation, or resemblance. It is even beyond mere relationality, and (con)formation. Claudia Welz holds that the created image is reference beyond itself—dynamic, as with a statue or icon, *and* symbolic—that is, indexical.

---

37. Welz, "Imago Dei," 87. For *Bildwissenschaft*, image theory, see Rampley, "Bildwissenschaft," 121.

38. Creasy Dean and Ron Foster, *The Godbearing Life*, cf. 141.

39. Auld, "Imago Dei in Genesis," 261. In 9:1, "said to them" is directed to Noah and his sons but not directly preceded by "and *God* said."

40. Welz, "Imago Dei," 82, emphasis mine.

According to the discipline of *Bildwissenschaft*, one must first understand "visual imagery as a communicative medium" to make a connection to God's first act toward the first human, that of direct speech. Communication with *hāādām* is the first revelation of God's self-hood. To image God is first to *be* a "communicative medium" (a "mouthpiece," a prophet). All the while the person is physically visible, acting out the glory of God: revealing God's righteousness, making things right in the world, being in right relationship.

Even the names ascribed to the members of the Trinity suggest communication. It is not just that the Messiah will be called Righteous. In Jeremiah 23:6, for example, the text says he will be called "the Lord is our Righteousness." That is to say, *Yahweh* is the unspeakable ״ (G-d); *Yahweh is*—in the act of being—our *Righteous-ness*, the state or condition of being righteous.[41] The righteousness and justice that reveal the character of God create, heal, rectify; reconcile us with ourselves; *and* are social—"put to right the disrupted relationships between people and nations [versus the reward or punishment of individuals]."[42] Trinitarian theology, according to Jürgen Moltmann, "starts from the interpersonal and communicative event of the acting persons about whom the biblical history of God tells."[43] To image the Trinity is to communicate and relate to one another.

What was lost, then, in the garden (Gen 2)? Do characteristics of being distinctly human still hint at characteristics of God's *ṣelem* and *dĕmût*? *Hāādām* was created in bodily form, so is it appropriate to understand human physical characteristics as clues to God's character? While Wolfhart Pannenberg promotes a critical appropriation of anthropology to theology,[44] he does find it acceptable "to lay theological claim to the human phenomena described in the anthropological disciplines."[45] At the same time, it must always be "provisional[,] . . . a version that needs to be

---

41. The subject of the degree to which a theologian can assert confidence in a Trinitarian model ("social trinity," Gunton, Moltmann, and their ilk; and von Balthasar's "theo-drama," etc.) is well catalogued. For a cogent argument for maintaining the mystery, see, Kilby, "Is an Apophatic Trinitarianism Possible?" 65–77.

42. Moltmann, *Sun of Righteousness, Arise!* 138–139.

43. Ibid., 149. For an exposition on Genesis 1 and the God who "acts by speaking," see Auld, "Imago Dei in Genesis," 259–62.

44. Pannenberg, *Anthropology in Theological Perspective*, 18. For a helpful critique of both Pannenberg's and Moltmann's eschatological Christology, see Harvie, "Living the Future," 149–64.

45. Pannenberg, *Anthropology in Theological Perspective*, 19.

expanded and deepened by showing that the *anthropological datum itself* contains a further and *theologically relevant* dimension."[46] The word "fall" is not used in Genesis 3, and sin language does not appear until the Cain narrative in Genesis 4:7.[47] It is non-communication, turning a deaf ear, that characterizes the deadening moment in the garden. They "heard the sound [voice] of God" (Gen 3:8) but hid themselves (i.e., closed their ears to the voice [presence, face] of God).[48] If the idea of relationship is what is highlighted, than "falling out" is more appropriate as a descriptor.[49] What is lost in the garden is intimate relationship with God, and, consequently, intimate relationship between the first two humans.

The redemptive work of Jesus makes possible the restoration of intimacy in human relationships—and images "the interpersonal and communicative event of the acting persons" of the Trinity. Thus, mindful attention to the voice of God evokes the created character of being human. That is, by being attentive to God, the person becomes attentive to others and makes right relationships that were perverted by the "falling out" in the garden.

By abiding in relationship with God and each other, human persons *live* the image of God. The indwelling Trinity that gives space to the Other is made visible in humankind when one intentionally pays attention to the other and is present without harsh judgment. To be present without harsh judgment is the very act of giving space to the other; by yielding, making room for the thoughts and feelings of the other, one becomes *more than*, and is more human. When a person gives kind attention in the present moment to another, attachment to one's own thought or perspective is suspended and open to change or augmentation. And herein lies the basis for group discernment: to give up space to another and thereby make room for something more.

KNOW GOD BY KNOWING EACH OTHER

God created humankind in God's image; in the image of God, they were created (Gen 1:27). At the same time, each person is unique and images God in a distinctive way. These distinctions give clues to the fullness of

46. Ibid., 20, emphasis mine.
47. Briggs, "Humans in the Image of God and Other Things Genesis Does Not Make Clear," 124.
48. Vogels, "It Is Not Good That the 'Mensch' Should Be Alone," 18.
49. Affirmed by Briggs quoting Terrence E. Fretheim in ibid., 125.

God's being, but when an unreflective disposition dominates—which is the "problem" presented in this thesis—the distinctions can be perverted, and relationships suffer. The most ostensible classification for human beings is that of male and female. So if understanding one another is helpful to understand and know God, understanding what it means to be male and female is crucial to an awareness of who God is.

Male and Female as Relationship

In the beginning, the first *adam* is created—both male and female. Together they image God—that is, as a relationship, they image God. The first thing that God tells them is "be fruitful and multiply, and fill the earth and subdue it; and have dominion over [it]" (Gen 1:28). The exhortation to make more humans is the only clue in the first creation narrative to the answer to the question, "why male and female?" Biologically they need each other to procreate. Besides that, the implication is that to subdue and have dominion over the earth is a group activity, not exclusively the provenance of being male or female. Participation in God's creation is relational and shared. And to see one another as *person* (versus merely man *or* woman) requires mindful attention, and curiosity about the individual beyond the difference in sex.

While there is a sense of sexual relationship implied in the exhortation to "be fruitful," it need not be laden with connotations of the lusty intercourse generally called to mind. The two phrases ("have dominion over" and "be fruitful") are so closely tied that the implication is more that bringing new human beings into the world is dependent on care for the land, and good stewardship over the land directly impacts the livelihood of those being born to it. In addition, as mentioned above, there are two places in the Old Testament that connect image and likeness in this way (Gen 1:26; 5:3). In both cases, the earth is vacant (in the first case, it is the beginning of all things; the second case directly follows the annihilation of humankind by the flood). The connection between image and likeness points to a notion that what constitutes being made in the image of God, distinctly human, is being more than one. And not only more than one; it is also to be in some type of covenantal relationship (marriage, accountability, parent-child, loyalty).

Stanley Grenz argues that sexuality "is the sense of incompleteness, together with the quest for wholeness. The eschatological community that

Biblical and Theological Foundation

is the goal of the creation of humankind as sexual creatures is not marriage per se, but the new humanity."[50] While Grenz implies that "sexuality" means difference in sex—i.e., male and female, where two people are required to co-procreate—"completeness" does not necessarily indicate a romantic entanglement or the act of sexual intercourse. Indeed, "[t]he relational self *is* sexual, [and] therefore, understood as *persons-in-bonded-community*. As such, the relational self is likewise the ecclesial self, the new humanity in communion with the triune God."[51] The point is the covenant*ing* relationship that is made possible through Christ between creation and the Creator, *and* between human beings.

In the Bible, the word for "female" (ûnᵉqēḇ≈āh) is only found in the opening creation narratives (Gen 1:27; 5:2) and in new beginnings—a reset, in the case of the pre- and post-flood narrative (Gen 6:19; 7:3, 9, 16). What is more, ûnᵉqēḇ≈āh is indicative of both lower animals and humankind. Again, it is only given in the context of beginnings. For the lower animals, however, the "be fruitful" is in a general, perpetual sense, while for *hāʾādām* it is the discrete, temporal sense.[52] Specifically, in Genesis 1:22, "multiply" (יִרֶב *yireḇ*) is the qal imperfect jussive (inferior as subject), for the birds of the air (and for the fish, to the filling point of the sea), but verse 1:28 uses "multiply" (. . .וּרְבוּ *uᵉrᵉḇuᵉ*), in the qal imperfect direct address. As such, it further emphasizes the creative element of *ᵉlōhîm* that *hāʾādām* images. What is more, in the direct address directly following "image" and "likeness," in verse 1:26, the creative act of multiplying may be indicative of God's nature, evidenced by the repeated coupling of "rule" and "multiply" in verses 26–28.[53]

As already detailed above, the priestly writer's use of *ᵉlōhîm* in the creation narrative carries with it the implication of plurality in the first human (as *imago dei*). Some theologians see the use of *ʾādām* (the first human) and *ʾādāmāh* (earth from which all creatures were made) as reflecting this notion. The usual "man," *ʾîsh* (found in the second, *Yahwist*, creation narrative), is not used to refer to one man, making the conclusion feasible. Towner concludes that the use of *ʾādām* instead of *ʾîsh* means that "for the Priestly writer both genders exist in this *ʾādām* from the outset."[54] Doubt-

---

50. Grenz, *The Social God and the Relational Self*, 19.
51. Ibid., 19, emphasis mine.
52. Bird, "Male and Female He Created Them," 153.
53. Gladd, "The Last Adam as the 'Life-Giving Spirit' Revisited," 299–300.
54. Towner, "Clones of God," 345.

less, far too much is made of the issue of gender with regard to *hāʾādām* and *ᵉlōhîm*. Those conversations miss the point and make humanity the focus. Furthermore, in the *Yahwist* account, the use of *kᵉ* for the "helper-partner/opposite" (*kᵉneg≈doʿ*) in 2:20 mirrors the "like the likeness" of 1:26, merely indicating copy, nothing more and nothing less, at least as regards gender.

The emphatic image and likeness ("like the likeness") points to the creation but reveals the Creator.[55] The chiastic referent, self-referent structure of verse 1:27 is strong evidence that God is not human, but distinguishing between (detailing) male and female indicates that the Creator possesses in some fashion aspects of being both male and female. The "created 'him'" (*ʾādām*, singular) is *both* male and female. And it is unclear what "male and female" signifies, for it is "the adam" (*hāʾādām*) that is created male and female. As *ṣalmû*, to image God "is not an objective representation of reality; it relates to the object as an extension and manifestation of divine *presence*."[56] Ultimately, what can be said is that to image God by being male and female humankind represents God's presence particularly when we are present to one another.

The Side Chamber: Rib

Another popular place to find the male-female delineation is in the second creation narrative in Genesis 2, where it describes the making of the second person by way of a "rib" taken from the first. Interestingly, the noun translated as "rib" in Genesis 2:21, צֵלָע (*ṣelaʿ*), is not translated in this way anywhere else in the Old Testament. What is more, this use is not substantiated in other ancient near east Hebrew literature texts. This is important to note, as this passage is often used to support the sublimation of women to a lesser status than that of men.

The noun is found in the inflected (function) thirteen times in the book of Exodus in nine verses (25:12; 26:20; 26:26; 26:27; 36:25; 36:31; 36:32; 37:3) in reference to temple construction and practice (e.g., placement of rings on the side of the altar; door placement at the side of the temple).[57] Beginning with 1 Kings 6:8, it is the "middle chamber," then

---

55. Gudbergsen, "God Consists of Both the Male and the Female Genders," 450–53.
56. Herring, "A 'Transubstantiated' Humanity," 486, emphasis mine.
57. Freedman, ed., *Eerdmans Dictionary of the Bible*. When Joshua 18:28 and 2 Samuel 21:14 use *ṣelaʿ*, it is the place name for one of the cities of the inheritance of Benjamin and the location where Saul and his son Jonathan were buried, respectively. And in 2

an isolated "stumble" in Jeremiah 20:10, and then again "side" or "middle chamber" in Ezekiel (Ezek 41:5; 41:6; 41:9; 41:11). It is also noteworthy that in the lemma (form) it is translated only as "side, middle chamber," or "middle story, side entrance."

Consider human anatomy. The area that would be deemed the middle chamber is the torso, or perhaps the womb. That is not to say that the first person was a female, nor that *hāʾādām* was androgynous, as is provocatively asserted by some.[58] Still, a second person clearly came from the abdomen of *hāʾādām*, and the image easily brings to mind a sort of birthing process. That God had to "close up the flesh" suggests the process was not the same kind of "birth" as the one that is most familiar, via the birth canal.

When God created humankind male and female, they were created through Christ ("through whom all things were created," John 1:3; Col 1:16; Rom 11:36), and one through the other. Then, each was given, "brought," to each other (Gen 2:22). They are part of each other ("bone" and "flesh") while distinctive; both are God's image bearers. By making one person out of another, the creative, life-giving character of God is made visible. Then, by coming together, two become more than two individuals. As male and female, the possibility exists for the creation of another person and for knowing God as creator of all life. Yet the relationship is also indicative of the act of giving oneself to the other in much the same way as God "breathed" God's life into the first human. The re-creative act in which the first two people engage reenacts the creative character of God. It is through creative activity, giving and receiving from each other, that two or more know God.

Mindfulness as Awareness of Self

Søren Kierkegaard suggested that the task of humankind is to become.[59] The task spans time while remaining individual. To become indicates process, an undertaking that requires reflection. Habitual immersion in daily activity is relatively mindless, and produces little, if any, change. With mindful attention, space is made for increasing the knowledge of who one

---

Samuel 16:13 *ṣelaʿ* refers to the slope/side of a hill. In the poetry of Psalms (35:15; 38:17) and Job 18:12, the word is translated three times as "stumble" or "fall." The root צלע gives us "lame" in Micah 4:6, 7; and Zephaniah 3:19.

58. Niskanen, "The Poetics of Adam," 419.

59. Pannenberg, Anthropology in Theological Perspective, 98.

is, the true person made in God's image. It is by orienting one's life around space and time for such reflection that it is possible to know one's self as *imago dei*.

Julian of Norwich's Mindful Practice

Julian of Norwich was an anchoress in fourteenth-century England. The role of an anchorite in the tradition of Anglican Christianity of that time was much like that of the monastics. Closed off from the daily activity of mainstream society, the anchorite spent much of the day in prayer and Scripture meditation. But unlike the monastics living in the desert or on the outskirts of the city, the anchorite stayed in a room attached to the local church and was available for counsel. This setting allowed Julian to spend two decades reflecting on revelations given to her by God concerning Jesus' crucifixion. Rather than immediately drawing conclusions at first glance, Julian spent time listening, lingering in relationship with God, who gave clarity to the visions and a deeper understanding of the character of Jesus.

The room in which Julian of Norwich lived was like a "side chamber" that birthed new revelations, like the "side chamber" that "birthed" a second human. And the revelations, or "showings," that Julian witnessed concerning the crucified Jesus revealed the new birth made possible through Jesus' side wound. These revelations were not mere dreaming, nor were they uncritically approached. Indeed, the theological development in Julian's reflections suggests the influence of Augustine and Thomas Aquinas, as well as Gregory and William of St. Thierry, in particular.[60] Research on Julian's *Revelations*, "with reference to the Latin theological authorities, especially Augustine, Bernard of Clarivaux, William of St Thierry and Bonaventure," determined statistically significant evidence of an explicit grasp of these theological authorities, as if Julian had read them in a systematic way.[61] By focusing intently on her crucified Lord, observing the copious outpouring of blood, and paying attention to Christ's side wound, Julian, assisted by the Spirit of God, gained comprehension of the divine Trinity in the act of Jesus's mutilated/ing body. This kind of participation in the *Perichoresis*, the revelation of the Trinity in the crucifixion, "finds an indigenous African parallel in *Ubuntu*, wherein our identity arises from

---

60. Jantzen, *Julian of Norwich*, 16–17.
61. Turner, "'Sin Is Behovely' in Julian of Norwich's *Revelations of Divine Love*," 408.

within community."⁶² Julian understood that she was participating in the divine creative–re-creative action, and clearly saw God not "as Being, but as the *act of Being* itself."⁶³ For Julian, recognizing the advent of "God is Love" obliges recognizing "a threesome: a Lover, a Beloved and the love that passes between them."⁶⁴ The whole of the revelation came to this: Love was his meaning.

Another primary (and recurrent) image that connects the anchorite to re-creative action is the correlation of the womb and the tomb. Indeed, the anchorite enters a room symbolic of the tomb after receiving extreme unction, while the womb offers a kind of double meaning, at once tomb-like and life-giving—a safe space to receive spiritual nutrition. So for Julian, the image of motherhood extends to all who are Christ's: "So our Lady is our mother, in whom we are all enclosed and born of her in Christ, for she who is mother of our savior is mother of all who are saved in our savior; and our savior is our true Mother, in whom all are endlessly born and out of whom we shall never come."⁶⁵ Herein lie hints of "through whom all things were birthed . . ." (John 1:3; Col 1:16). The sacrifice of Jesus, the mutilation and bloodletting of the divine-human body, is an eternal manifestation of God's unbounded love. It is a lived reality that humanity is welcomed into—but they must enter through the wound (side chamber) and be absorbed. Entering that space, "to become that space—where thinking otherwise can happen; where creative responses to the deathly structures of modernity can be discerned," is the means by which they might be enacted, and be "endlessly born."⁶⁶

Julian's reference to Christ as Mother was not unique in the fourteenth century. Seepage from orifices, wetness, is ascribed to women, while dryness, strength, heat, etc., were male characteristics in the common thought of the time.⁶⁷ In addition, breast milk was believed to be derivative of blood,

---

62. Charleton, *Non-Dualism in Eckhart, Julian of Norwich and Traherne*, 4640–4642, Kindle.

63. Ibid., 2812. For a contemporary and more formally theological treatment of act-as-being, see Gunton, *Act & Being*.

64. Ibid., 2808.

65. Ibid.

66. Jantzen, *Julian of Norwich*, xx–xxi. "Entering the wound" is a theme found in much of Charles Wesley's hymnody. See "Wesley Hymn Collection," Northwest Nazarene University.

67. Ambrose of Milan speaks of God the Father as having breasts and a womb; Anselm addresses the image of Christ as mother; Bernard of Clarivaux and William of St.

so the leap from Christ's blood as nourishment in the drama of the Eucharist is easy to make. Still, Julian does not employ (exploit) gender to inform this image of Christ; indeed, she goes on to describe this Christ Mother as one who fiercely loves in all wisdom—characteristics credited only to men during the late Medieval era. What is more, Julian does not see only the mother and not father. She clearly identifies both titles, affirming that God is neither male nor female but *is* who God *is*—entirely. At the same time, "it is specifically through motherhood that humanity is drawn into relationship with the Triune God and brought to its own wholeness."[68] It is not that Christ *acts* like a mother, but that "to know Christ as mother is to know 'the very nature of God.'"[69] Julian recognizes "[God] is the ground, he is the substance, he is kind nature itself and he is true father and true mother of nature."[70] Indeed, the Council of Toledo in 675 stated: "We must believe that the Son was not made out of nothing, nor out of some substance or other, but *from the womb* of the Father (*de utero Patris*)."[71] To attribute to God literal fatherhood is to occasion idolatry. Emphasizing either fatherhood or motherhood, though, is another way to understand the relational reality of the Trinity within itself, between the Trinity and humanity, and amidst humanity.

The Trinity is revealed in Jesus' humanity on the cross, the eternal redemptive will that is love. And in Christ's body, all who will be saved can gaze on it and see heaven. To understand the power of Christ's blood and the breadth, the immensity, of its capacity to atone, God showed Julian that the blood is human blood, while absolutely suffused with the *generative* power of his divinity. This "human blood that harrows hell, that 'overflows all the earth, and is ready to wash from sin all creatures that are, have been, and will be of good will,' and that ascends in Christ's body into heaven," is infinite in its fecundity and power to redeem.[72] Julian could thus see that sin is nothing ("noughting"). Though sin is not itself an act, we know the effects of it by the pain it causes, and this pain is evidenced "preeminently" on the cross, degraded, received, and soaked into the very earth from which *hā'ādām* was made, making it, again, well. The power of Satan is overtaken,

---

Thierry refer to nursing from the breasts of Christ.

68. Reinhard, "Joy to the Father, Bliss to the Son," 630.
69. Ibid., 632.
70. Ibid.
71. Byassee, "Closer Than Kissing," 150.
72. Bauerschmidt, *Julian of Norwich and the Mystical Body Politic of Christ*, 85.

leaving no space for evil. In fact, "Satan's power is shown to be... 'vnmyght [unmight].'... God's power is not one that must struggle for dominance over other powers, or one that has delimitable sphere proper to it that it might seek to expand.... [It is] not so much a defeat as an *unmasking* of demonic pretensions."[73] The truth of God's presence and power revealed by the cross destroys the façade that sin erected to cover the truth of the character of humankind created in God's image.

In the third showing, Julian saw that "all things that are done are done well, for our lord God does all... for he is the midpoint of all things, and all that he does,"... so, "sin is not an action." Evil cannot even be considered a deed "in relationship to God's activity."[74] God's action on creation is not a new event, but "*creatio ex nihilo* played, if you will, in another key." And so, Julian can say, "for just as the blessed Trinity created all things from nothing, just so shall the same blessed Trinity make well all that is not well."[75]

Julian's intention is to communicate this divine message to all; her revelations are meant for all people. Julian is a lover of the Triune God, and the approach to God and revelation from God ("showings") is prayer. She sees the compassion of Christ as "a hollowing out of the self; it is 'mynde of his blessyd passion,' in which one's suffering is displaced by Christ, who is possessed of all of creation's suffering."[76] Julian plainly sees the will and being of Jesus on the cross not as an event but as *time and space suspended* for whatever span is required, that "all who would be saved" are enfolded into the suffering/"ever-naughting" flesh. Christ suspends time to encompass those who would be saved. It is in suspending time, making space, that creation might know Christ revealed within.

When Christ's side is opened, the wound is available for humanity to reenter and be born anew. Jesus' death on the cross is the ultimate example of giving self to another (all others). The side wound becomes both the entrance into resurrected life and into the power of Jesus' redemptive work, and the exit that birthing evokes. Through the "showings," Julian comes to understand who she is as enfolded into Christ's suffering whereby her own suffering is made inert. In viewing Christ's passion, Julian can see that evil is no longer relevant and is able to view her own grief with a "holy indifference," that is, to suspend harsh judgment and to see how things actually are

73. Ibid., emphasis mine.
74. Ibid., 98.
75. Ibid., 99.
76. Ibid., 106.

by Christ's intervention. The side wound of Christ correlates with the side (ṣelaʿ) of the first Adam, at once a place of redemption and of new life. The side wound is the place where Julian finds herself being redeemed and the vessel through which God might show this redemption to another, ushering new life.

Mindfulness as Awareness of Self in Relationship to Other

A feature that makes human beings human is the "capacity for objectivity." Humans are present, but they are also capable of perceiving the past and future (Eccl 3:11)—in other words, they have the ability to be self-distancing and objective. This means that humans also have the capacity to be present to another *as* other. To be human is to be "present to *what is other than themselves*."[77] For Wolfhart Pannenberg, sin distorts this natural order, and is the "failure of human beings in relation to themselves." It is a self-love, a distortion of humanness that does not trust in the Other with whom one must be related in order to be fully (whole-ly) human.

To disrupt this presence to each other and to an Other disrupts a full identification with self-as-human. Sin has been variously defined as a "quarrel with the self" (Plessner), "disunity of self" (Dieter Wyss), "concupiscence" (Augustine),[78] shortsightedness, ego, and succumbing to the vital/instinctual that sees desire for and as need—desire for its own sake.[79] For Kierkegaard, "the spirit is the self" and by relating only to the self, the relation to the Spirit of God is severed, leading to despair. Modern individualism sees self as already *as-is,* still in need of collation "to be achieved by themselves and *as* themselves."[80] But it is an "illusion that the synthesis which is the self must be the act of an already existing subject and a creation of its freedom."[81] The idea that freedom is self-enacted and that to be human is self-reflexive is an illusion.

For Barth, the essence of the Triune deity is revelation-in-act (versus proposition). That is, "God *is* who God *is* revealed to be."[82] In this way, the

77. Pannenberg, *Anthropology in Theological Perspective*, 61.

78. *Concupiscence* is sometimes the punishment (consequence) for sin, in Augustine, and other times a sin itself. Hence, the difficulty in interpreting. See ibid., 87.

79. Ibid., 89.

80. Ibid., 100.

81. Ibid., 101.

82. Grenz, *The Social God and the Relational Self,* 35.

doctrine comes from revelation rather than exclusively the philosophical. Similarly, Jürgen Moltmann acknowledges that "the cross is not only the event that effects human reconciliation but [it is] also the occasion of God's act of self-constitution within history as the triune one."[83] Mindfulness that acknowledges relationship with an Other reflects on the spirit in relation to the Spirit of God. This same Spirit relates to the spirit of all created in God's image. It is by being present to another *as* other that a person might expand the capacity for seeing another as the other person truly is. And it is by seeing another person *as* the other person truly is that one expands in one's capacity to more fully see God for who God is.

The importance of knowing oneself and others is evident in God's creative and redemptive acts. By making humankind male and female, God created beings who would necessarily be in relationship with each other. When the first people made a decision apart from God, as when Eve ate the fruit without consulting with God (Gen 3:1–7), the text says, "their eyes were opened." In truth, this blinded each to the other as they were. The differences in body, in flesh, became a barrier to relating in perfect unity—a "disunity of self." Stripped of clothing and, ultimately, life, Christ created the possibility for sight into the self and other without shame when God's Spirit could enter—indwell—"all who would be saved."

There is an obvious functional aspect to humankind being made as male and female. Together, a man and woman are capable of making another human being, and this act certainly reflects the character of the Creator of all life. Still, God's exhortation to "multiply and fill the earth" (Gen 1:28) is provisional. The bodily shame that resulted from the disunity was not just in regard to each other, but in regard to God as well (Gen 3:10). There is physical difference between man and woman, but in regards to, " . . . subdu[ing] [the earth] and hav[ing] dominion over the fish of the sea and over the birds of the air and over every living thing that moves upon the earth" (Gen. 1:28), *male* and *female* is irrelevant. The life given via the side chamber and the new life given by way of the side wound make viable flawless vision beyond the difference in fleshly appearance. In this way one is fully known, and can know oneself and one another. To have dominion is to lead in this world unbounded by the shame made evident by shortsightedness. Mindful discernment in solitude and with others expands the capacity to know God and others, and in so doing, know oneself.

83. Ibid., 42.

KNOW GOD BY KNOWING ANOTHER CULTURE

Each person is unique and images God in a distinctive way. Just as gender is an obvious distinguishing characteristic, so can ethnicity and race set one individual apart from another.[84] And, for many of the same reasons as with gender, these distinctions, when unconsidered, can be used for harm. It was only when Peter, as described in Acts 10, spent time in quiet reflection ("prayer") that he could see the possibility for fellowship with a Gentile.[85] And it was only when the apostles were together observing Pentecost (a time of corporate reflection on Israel's deliverance by God from Egypt) that others from many nations could hear God's words in their "*native* language" (Acts 2:8). What they heard was not just a translation from the Greek or Aramaic; rather, the message was heard in the idiom and inflection of the language of their respective cultures. God becomes known in every nation, every culture.

Jew and Greek, All Nations

Every person is created as an object of God's mindful attention in equal measure. Each person is also unique and expresses a distinctive aspect of God's image. Diversity makes possible a broader understanding of God, but difference can also be a source of misunderstanding and discord. Full knowledge of one who is different and greater unity are both possible when one yields space to another. Similarly, a broader perception of God increases the potential for a greater range of expressed image and likeness of God.

Concerns pertaining to race and gender overlap and are highlighted in Galatians 3:28. Chinese biblical scholar Lung-kwong Lo highlights Paul's evident concern for unity (versus the often implied erasure of ethnic identity).[86] Lo explains that the *Pax Romana* was a similar venue to the current "glocalization": the "small-world" phenomenon of increasingly easy access to the world alongside the need to address local ethnic issues escalating

---

84. This thesis may be limited by the cultural bias of the researcher and research tools; a complete theology of culture is beyond its scope. For a cogent perspective on *cultural* perspective see, for example, Chow, "I Insist on the Christian Dimension," 224–49.

85. I am grateful to John Anderson, DMin adjunct professor at Denver Seminary, for making the connection of cultural overlap in the book of Acts during a phone conversation, March 25, 2015.

86. Lo, "'Neither Jew nor Greek': Galatians 3:28 Revisited," 25–33.

in significance.[87] Theological discussion has traditionally interpreted the letter of Galatians as theological (versus sociopolitical). But saying that the first Christians were to do away with previous religious practices in order to enjoy unity has real, practical, social concerns. For Lo, Paul is not indicating that there are no longer expressed differences between male and female, Greek and Jew, slave and free. What he seems to be advocating for is equal regard toward each other in the midst of difference.[88]

Respect and even celebration of the difference of the other is obvious to most post-modern, post-colonial theologians. Yet the practice of such unity in diversity is not very enjoyable when the group as a whole is merely exhorted to respect the other. Tolerance and acceptance have become key terms in education policy and politics in general. Conspicuously absent, however, is the sense that the other (individual, culture, people group, tradition) expresses an aspect of God's character and God's image in a unique way. To simply accept the difference that exists is really to dismiss it and, in effect, consider it less important. When difference is merely accepted and is not considered a revelation of God's image, then difference is incidental, and a person who is not seen to be crucially revealing God's image may easily be exploited. To see the image and likeness of God in the other is to recognize the Spirit, the same Spirit indwelling all peoples who are created in that image. To see the image and likeness of God in the other is to notice the unique character of the gifts given—of which there are "many" (1 Cor 12:4–11)—and honor them, glorify them . . . for the building up in love, in the body of Christ, for maturity (Eph 4:1–15).

Moltmann makes clear, "This is not a premodern eulogy of a uniform unity, nor is it a postmodern glorification of diversity. The hierarchical church distinguished between priests and laity. The christocentric church made all free and equal as brothers and sisters." It is power via "the divine Spirit which [sic] confers *community in diversity*."[89] It is not expressed as "power above them," or the "ground beneath them," but as a "bond between them!" The character of the Trinity, whose image humankind bear, is bonding between members of a diverse community. A bond is possible only when each member willingly makes space for the other and gives up power

---

87. Ibid. One need not look far in the United States to notice local issues of ethnic diversity, from immigration legislation and terrorist extremism to the urban "war on drugs" and the system of incarceration.

88. Lo, "'Neither Jew nor Greek': Galatians 3:28 Revisited," 30.

89. Moltmann, *Sun of Righteousness, Arise!* 24–25, emphasis mine.

so the powerless might be empowered. By suspending one's individual perspective—making space—it is possible to see and hear the perspective of another culture and be enlightened and empowered by more of God.

The Interpretive Lens

History demonstrates that one of the ways difference in culture (or race or religion) is addressed is by conquering a group of people and bending them to mimic the dominant culture. A frequent result is the stamping out of the divine character of the colonized peoples and effectually quenching the Spirit that breathed fresh life into that culture. It also serves to overemphasize and pervert the God-created aspect of the dominant culture to an often-unrecognizable extent. This is Israel's experience during much of its history. Interpreting Scripture through the eyes of such peoples (versus through the eyes of the chief western-European male perspective that dominates the bulk of Christian theological history) expands the view of God and the view of the other.

Language and culture give meaning, at once revealing unique aspects of God's character and limiting the range of vision to see and understand God's character revealed in the other. Too often in history, Christianity colonized people and crushed their *imago dei* by imposing a foreign, incongruent culture. Liberation and feminist theology address this cultural colonialism by utilizing alternative interpretative lenses. In this tradition, feminist theology use similar lenses to revise interpretations of what is meant by "male and female God created them" (Gen 1:27).

Postcolonial lenses reject colonial interests and engage in emancipatory reading by exposing the "colonial codes" that support colonial ideologies. Postcolonial readings are, in essence, a search for "oppositional or protest voices"[90] that seek a different vision for humans created in God's image. "The construction of race and ethnicity of minority groups often is done by the dominant culture and colonial power," not to understand but to dominate others.[91] Minority women struggle against two dominant interpretations: liberationist readings of imperialism *and* feminist readings of patriarchy (Musa Dube[92]).

90. Kuan and Tran, "Reading Race Reading Rahab, 29.
91. Ibid.
92. Dube Shomanah, *Postcolonial Feminist Interpretation of the Bible*, 26. For a more academic postcolonial feminist theology see Kwok, *Postcolonial Imagination and*

Asian American theologians Jeffrey K. Kuan and Mai-Anh Le Tran demonstrate the process by reading the narrative of Rahab in Joshua 2 for a "feminist postcolonial dialogical/cross-textual" reading in four tropes: (1) hybridity and liminality, (2) yellow peril/perpetual foreigner, (3) model minority, and (4) sexualized other.[93]

Essentially, hybrid-liminality is living in the in-between, not fully one or the other (e.g., not Asian nor American). Rahab knows her own people (though, as a prostitute, she would not know her clients' names). Rahab also knows the Israelites—their deity's name, purpose, and history. Thus she speaks both "languages."[94] The physical location is the wall, that is, the liminal space.

The "perpetual foreigner" is the American with an Asian face, continually being asked, "where are you *really* from?" The question is always present—even for second, third, fourth (and on) generations. Rahab, too, is the "quintessential outsider": a woman, a prostitute, a Canaanite. As a "betrayer," she becomes an "insider" while remaining perpetually foreign, "ironically . . . in her own land."[95] She is a member of the community while not quite belonging to it.

The "model minority" among Asian Americans, for example, is characterized as "intelligent, gifted in math and science, polite, hard working, family oriented, law abiding, and successful entrepreneurial."[96] But the Asian American (or other model minorities) is often a pawn in the dominant culture's racism, pitted against, for example, African and Hispanic cultures. Rahab, for her part, is the model proselyte. She is characterized as "intelligent and knowledgeable . . ., economically independent . . ., resourceful . . ., an entrepreneur and a good negotiator."[97] All this, and yet she rejects other gods and remains faithful to Yahweh.

Dominant characters are also generalized onto Asian American women in the category of the "sexualized other": "geisha girl," "mail-order

---

Feminist Theology, 55.

93. Kuan and Tran, "Reading Race Reading Rahab," 30.

94. Ibid., 32–33.

95. Ibid., 34–35. Her situation evokes the Native American experience. For a cogent treatment of one First Nations' perspective, see Layoun, *Wedded to the Land?*. For a theological/political application to the Native plight, see Tinker, *Spirit and Resistance*.

96. Kuan and Tran, "Reading Race Reading Rahab," 37.

97. Ibid., 38–39.

bride," "dragon lady," "lotus blossom," etc.[98] Moreover, Asian women are characterized as "servile, compliant, self-sacrificing, exotically sensual, masochistic, or 'desirous of sexual domination.'"[99] Rahab's name, *rāhāb*, means "broad," likely in the sense of sexual experience. The meaning is easily recognized in Joshua 2:3: "Bring out the men who entered you (*habba'im 'elayik*), who entered your house." The implication is that they received sexual favors from her; the crimson cord she ties to the window is a sexual allusion "linked to prostitution, promiscuity, or eroticism."[100] The Jewish biblical scholar Tikva Frymer-Kensky "refers to Rahab as 'this biblical Suzie Wong.'"[101] The red cord hanging out of the window—as the "scarlet letter 'A'" in Nathaniel Hawthorne's novel—becomes "hung as a proud sign of salvation in the midst of or in spite of cultural condemnation." Entering her house is "an act of sexual conquest," a premier of the city's conquest.[102] By reading the Joshua passage through a cultural lens that is different from traditional, European, male-centric theologies, understanding of God's message is expanded.

The larger concern may be that sexualization is a dominant issue clouding nearly every interpretive lens. This is especially evident by the use of sexualized themes in virtually all media, and the scale and reach of the pornography industry. However, in deciphering the meaning of the priestly creation narrative concerning the *imago dei* comprising '*ādām*, male *and* female, wiping the interpretive lens of bias as much as possible is ideal in the very least. But the interpretive lens cannot be cleared without making time and space for reflection and mindful attention to the other. And the greater the difference, the more time and space are required.

In Our Own Language

Difference can be distinguished by gender and is seen between races and cultures. Difference is also highlighted in social structure, such as through the conferment of a title by education or holy orders. And yet the same Spirit that spoke at Pentecost to all peoples in their own idioms speaks to all who pray, with the priesthood belonging to all who believe (1 Pet 2:5).

98. Ibid., 40.
99. Ibid.
100. Ibid.
101. Frymer-Kensky, *Reading the Women of the Bible*.
102. Kuan and Tran, "Reading Race Reading Rahab," 40.

Biblical and Theological Foundation

One Spirit spoke to many people groups in a variety of languages and in the idioms with which each could understand God's meaning. It is in this very act of the Spirit in the context of prayer that social structure can be seen for what it is and whom it serves. When a disparate group of people pray together, the same Spirit hears their prayers and unmasks the façade that social structures make in service to categorization.

Language shapes and is shaped by culture. Each language-culture images God in a unique way, so to know God better is to understand and know one another. Pannenberg expands, "Just as no concept is possible without language, so too 'the whole range of subjective perception of objects' finds expression in language; consequently, 'every language contains a characteristic view of the world.'"[103] Each language, each culture, has a unique worldview expressing an equally unique aspect of God's character. These differences have been illustrated in comparisons between Hebrew and Greek thought. A debate arising from arguments developed by Bruno Snell (on Greek thought) and Thorlief Boman (on Hebrew thought) suggests that nuance of language, speech, and structure influence perspective and even the process of thought, which all impacts identity and culture.[104] What is more, language changes over time. For example, Irenaeus replaced the Greek word "covering," in 1 Corinthians 11, with "veil," which continues to be used in many translations today.[105] Dictionaries expand with new words coined, and old words acquire new meanings. There remain "shifts in the meanings of words and thus in the associations linked with such words."[106] Changes within languages reflect the process of individual becoming. Static interpretations can be used inappropriately as a power tool for control and to limit change.

---

103. Pannenberg, *Anthropology in Theological Perspective*, 343. See von Humboldt, *Über die Verschiedenheiten des menschlichen Sprachbaues* (1827–29), 191. The impact of language development on attitudes and learning is further explored in chapter three.

104. For a discussion on the degree of significance, if any, in difference in thought process based on language of origin (i.e., Hebrew versus Greek) see, Pannenberg, *Anthropology in Theological Perspective*, 343–345.

105. Campbell and Torrance, *Gospel and Gender*, 49. For a more current (provocative) translation/interpretation, see Thiselton, "The Significance of Recent Research on 1 Corinthians," 320–52.

106. Pannenberg, *Anthropology in Theological Perspective*, 344. Equally so, biblical language influences interpretation, as does the development of language over time, which changes the understanding of its meaning. It must be taken in its current and historical context.

Noam Chomsky insists there is a "universal generative transformational grammar that transcends the differences between the individual languages."[107] And yet, while we can think without words (e.g., introspection), thinking is not "independent of language."[108] It is unquestionably nuanced and complex. Language and culture inform the identity of an individual and reflect aspects of God's character. Individuals and cultures are influenced by language, while language develops around a transforming culture. And while the variety of languages challenges cross-cultural communication, there is an aspect of being human that transcends language and speaks directly to the soul, as when God said . . . and it was so. In some measure, language can articulate meaning. To understand the meaning, mindful attention to God's revelation within it is crucial.

The Same Spirit

The mindfulness practice of prayer deepens the relationship between practitioner and the Spirit of God. In this mindful exchange, it is possible to know the mind of Christ (1 Cor 2). The power to discern what is right and good, then, is "subject to no one else's scrutiny" (1 Cor 2:15). At the same time, the corrective to "pray as we ought" (Rom 8:26) occurs in the context of accountable community, which is the group mindfulness practice of discernment. It is through deep prayer, by the leading efficacy of the Spirit and in increasing union with Christ, that the community of believers can know and become more like God.

The group mindfulness practice of discernment opens the individual and community to better grasp what it means to bear God's image. One passage that is instructive concerning the *imago dei* but is typically overlooked on that topic is chapter eight of Romans. According to systematic theologian Sarah Coakley, the neglect is seen nearly from the outset of Christianity. It seems to have been lost in a misguided focus on the perceived difference between so-called Eastern and Western theologies. A recent surge of literature reassessing the development of Trinitarian theology sheds light on "earlier (and demonstrably false) disjunction between East and West, which has indeed beguiled the systematicians for much of the twentieth century."[109] Conventional interpretations historically see a polar-

---

107. Ibid., 344–345.
108. Ibid., 346.
109. Coakley, "Introduction: Disputed Questions in Patristic Trinitarianism," 128.

Biblical and Theological Foundation

ity between East and West conceptions of the Person(hood) of the Trinity, and see psychological constructs in, for instance, Augustine's view. However, Coakley notes that "Augustine's vision of the self is already rooted in the Trinitarian God, and thus . . . the structure of the human mind can only be made known *through the Trinity.*" With this rebuke for reading modern psychology into Augustine, it is possible to recognize that he employed analogies of personhood "as indicators of the self's being made precisely in the imago Dei (the image of the Trinity), and engaged restlessly in search of divine transformation and salvation in relation to that Trinity."[110]

The above-mentioned historically perceived dichotomy stemmed from an over-focus on one Person of the Trinity over Another, and on that Person's authority as being greater than the Others. For example, Romans 8:9–30 is an "invitation to the pray-er to be drawn by an intervention of the Spirit into an intimate incorporation into the life Christ."[111] By recognizing prayer as such, this approach exegetically gives special authority to the Spirit. By contrast, John's *Logos* emphasizes the Son's authority by way of the Father. Because the discussion in those first centuries, as much as now, cannot be reduced to strictly antithetical viewpoints, it would be disingenuous to suggest a single factor caused the oversight. Still, the topic of intercessory prayer significantly impacted the "social location increasingly in tension . . . with the episcopal jurisdiction in the post-Constantinian period."[112] The politics of church and state evidenced then as now. Montanism,[113] for one, was a significant concern of the time.

Whatever the case, Coakley sees a second-century "fork in the theological path."[114] As mentioned above, the task for second- and third-century church leaders was to clearly articulate and define the parameters of Christian doctrine. On the one hand, "Orthodoxy," for Origen, was "a goal-directed project of spiritual transformation; it is not acquired or guaranteed by creedal ascent, nor backed up by hierarchical authority."[115] Coak-

---

110. Ibid., 134. Coakley summarizes Drever's analyses of Ayers' work.

111. Coakley, "Prayer, Politics and the Trinity," 380.

112. Ibid., 381.

113. So named after second-century Montanus, who, along with others of the so-called New Prophecy, believed the Spirit continued to give special revelation to the church, and specifically to him. For a succinct overview and relationship to present-day Pentecostal movements, see Robeck Jr., "Montanism and Present Day 'Prophets,'" 413–29.

114. Coakley, "Prayer, Politics and the Trinity," 383.

115. Ibid., 388.

ley sees what historians coined the "Origenist crisis," beginning in 399 CE and represented by Theophilus of Alexandria, as stemming less from a true accusation of heresy than from *politics* and from the issue of the "sacramental role as Bishop." That is, the crisis was wrought by "different forms of *theological* power."[116] In particular, it was "episcopal/sacramental power versus monastic/pneumatological power." Theophilus, for his part, sought to capture the power-as-prayer while seeking to censure it, venerating it while "fearing its potential capacity for institutional destabilisation [sic]."[117] It is important to reiterate that the "crisis" was not a brawl between "charisma and institution." Rather, the issue was one of power and control, with the "sacramental institution attempting to harness and own the irreducible power of personal prayer."[118] And to treat the gift of the Spirit as an élite method is to limit the relationship between Spirit and leader, and between the Spirit and the people.

In this way, the first people restricted the relationship between God and themselves. Turning a deaf ear to God's voice in the garden of Eden deprived the body of oxygen, since "the Spirit is life because of righteousness" (Rom 8:10b). The work of Christ made it possible for the Breath of life to revive the body: "If the Spirit of him who raised Jesus from the dead dwells in you, he who raised Christ from the dead will give life to your mortal bodies also through his Spirit that dwells in you" (Rom 8:11). Making things right and just by sharing power—because the power is Love, the Spirit of God—is righteousness and life. Origen beautifully imagined the role of the Spirit in (re)creative life by speaking metaphorically about barrenness and conception, birthing and fruitfulness: "it is when Christians 'perceive the sterility of their own governing reason and the barrenness of their own mind' that 'through persistent prayer they conceive from the Holy Spirit ... words filled with visions of the truth; and they give birth to them' (13.3; see also 13.4)."[119] Origen was careful to distinguish spiritual insight from

---

116. Ibid., 394.

117. Ibid.

118. Ibid., 398.

119. Coakley, "Prayer, Politics and the Trinity," 385. Sarah Coakley is the Norris-Hulse Professor of Divinity and holds the established chair at Cambridge in philosophy of religion, specializing in the patristic, scholastic, and contemporary doctrine of the Trinity. The only modern edition of the Greek remains *Origenes Werke*, vol. 2, 297–403. Coakley utilizes the translation in *Origen*, tr. Greer, Classics of Western Spirituality, 81–170.

Biblical and Theological Foundation

ecstatic frenzy associated with mostly physical and sometime erotic exhibition, as well as the demonic.

Like Origen, Athanasius understood the role of the Spirit as relational and personal. But, it was not until after Athanasius' exile to the desert by the fifth century that he began writing about the role of the Spirit as one of the Trinity.[120] Mindful attention in quiet space in the context of the community of monks left Athanasius open to understanding God in a new way. While Athanasius asserts *imago dei* was entirely lost at the Fall, creating an "ontological gulf" between humans and God, he insisted that those who believe could embody the Spirit. Pope Theophilus levied accusations against this Origenist emphasis on the Spirit's incorporation and transformative power, despite his "Homily on Repentance" that taught repentance as a means "that makes the Holy Spirit quickly enter into you and take up his abode in you."[121] These contradictions make evident the fact that the "crisis" was about maintaining ecclesial power and control rather than orthodoxy.

The goal for Pope Theophilus was not to eliminate the role of the Spirit in the believer but rather to "tame and utilize its force."[122] Leadership and power, theology and ecclesia, are complex relationships. Coakley concludes that church history illustrates "that the Romans 8 approach to the Trinity (through deep prayer, by the leading efficacy of the Spirit, and in increasing union with Christ) brings its exponents into the danger of at least some tension with ecclesiastical authority."[123] It is likely there will continue to be tension in relationship with those who sit in that authority. Romans 8 reveals that all have access to the mind of Christ, not merely a select few. At the same time, greater clarity occurs when individuals discern the mind of Christ in the context of a community.

For Coakley, "Christian prayer is not meant to be a distant relationship between two fixed entities—one named 'God' and the other 'creature'—but rather a 'movement of divine reflexivity, a sort of answering of God to God in and through the one who prays (Rom 8:26–27).'"[124] To pray is to participate in the Trinity, and, in doing so, image the Triune God:

> [This] profound, though often fleeting or obscure, sense of entering in prayer into a "conversation" already in play, a reciprocal

---

120. Coakley, "Prayer, Politics and the Trinity," 390.
121. Ibid., 396.
122. Ibid., 398.
123. Ibid., 399.
124. Quoted in Byassee, "Closer Than Kissing," 142.

divine conversation between Father and Spirit which can finally be reduced neither to divine monologue nor human self-transcendence, is our best scriptural description of an irreducibly triune experience.[125]

The act of prayer *is* imaging God. The act of prayer is imaging by participating, as the Spirit with the human spirit attests: we belong. Christ, giving up, emptying himself—*kenosis*—is an act of the Trinity, a making space for God. It is giving up space to be filled and give again to each other. The Spirit that raised Jesus from the dead is the same Spirit that dwells in each who is saved (Rom 8:11). This same Spirit "is witness with our spirit" (Rom 8:16), making possible sight beyond the flesh—which once brought shame—to the work and life of the Spirit in another. "'Self-emptying' is not a negation of self, but the place of the self's transformation and expansion into God."[126] C. F. D. Moule restates: "Jesus displayed the self-giving humility which is the *essence of divinity*."[127] Jesus gave up space, his divinity, to make space for humankind so that humanity might participate in the divine.

That Jesus gave up his power is a summons to Christian leaders to do the same. The *New Oxford American Dictionary* defines discernment as "perception in the absence of judgment with a view to obtaining spiritual direction and understanding."[128] To make space for another is to relinquish judgment and preconception based on the superfluous, the external flesh that was the original object of shame. To give space to one who is different in gender or culture is to allow that space to be filled by another perspective. The giver is now filled by the possibility of a broader view, a richer understanding of an issue at hand. The exchange is transformative, creating a space to expand into God.

Many Gifts, One Spirit

There is diversity in gender, in culture and race, and in social status. There is also diversity in spiritual gifts—personal gifts and leadership gifts. The fourth chapter of Ephesians explains some of the gifts that are particular to effective leadership. Alongside the descriptions is an instruction: since the Source is one Spirit, unity is critical, and to be expected. And once again,

125. Ibid.
126. Coakley, *Powers and Submissions*, 36.
127. Quoted in ibid., 10.
128. *New Oxford American Dictionary*.

Biblical and Theological Foundation

discernment of how the variety of gifts work together in a certain setting or circumstance is augmented by mindful awareness of each other and the Spirit of God. The text also indicates that discerning the use of these gifts in unity is most effective for moving toward maturity "to the measure of the full stature of Christ" (Eph 4:13) with renewed sensitivity to the Spirit that was previously lost (v. 19).

The letter to the Ephesians functions as an admonition to the church to maintain focus on its identity as incorporated into Christ. The letter is unique in its exclusive focus "on identity and [construction] around five explicit 'formerly-now' contrasts (2:1–10; 2:11–13; 2:19–22; 4:17–24; and 5:8)."[129] As with Galatians and the epistle to the Hebrews, the recipients of Ephesians were concerned about a sort of return to the forms of Judaism.[130] Rüdiger Fuchs suggests that, to serve as a corrective, the content of the letters and circulars attributed to Paul shifts to a greater emphasis on Christology. The use of "in Christ" increases from the accepted ealier work to the later epistles. In Galatians (the clear message of which is to emphasize that *all* are "in Christ"), the phrase is mentioned eight times, but in Ephesians the occurrence jumps to thirty-four occurrences.[131]

To be "in Christ" is fundamental to Christian identity, as individuals and as the church. The phrase is correlated to Hebrews 1:3,[132] which explains that Jesus is "the exact imprint of God's very being." The implications of Christ as imprint are explained in chapter two of Hebrews: "the one who sanctifies [Jesus] and [the ones] who are sanctified all have one Father" (v. 11); as Jesus is "now crowned with glory and honor" (v. 9), God has now "crowned [humanity] with glory and honor" (v. 7). The word for "exact imprint," χαρκτήρ (*charaktēr*) [GNT-TIS], (translated "character"; "express image") is not used in this way (inflected, lemma) anywhere else in the New Testament.[133] As the perfect *imago dei*, Christ is the perfect revelation of

---

129. Snodgrass, "Paul's Focus on Identity," 262.

130. MacLeod, "The Finality of Christ," 211.

131. Fuchs, "I Kneel Before the Father and Pray for You (Ephesians 3:14)," 16. Maintaining unity in the bond of peace exhorted in Ephesians 4:3 is affirmed in psychology: "According to both positive psychology and Scripture, harmony between people from different backgrounds is a desirable goal but one that requires hard relational work." Entwistle and Moroney, "Integrative Perspectives on Human Flourishing," 295–303.

132. Mackie, "Confession of the Son of God," 446.

133. The root is found in only ten other instances; three are discrete uses, and the remaining seven are in the book of Revelation: Luke 19:43, χάρακά χάραξ "barricade, bulwark" (NRSVS), translated "ramparts"; Acts 17:29 χαράγματι χάραγμα "mark, stamp,"

God—a renewal of the human image of God and a sign of its eschatological fulfillment. Christ is the image of God that is expressed/experienced communally in the church. Therefore, to be "in Christ," the one who is "the exact imprint of God's very being," carries enormous implications for the degree to which humankind reflects "God's very being."

Ephesians, especially verse 4:3, "making every effort to maintain the unity of the Spirit in the bond of peace," features prominently in the addresses given at denominational general conferences, missionary sessions, and international symposiums. It is understandable that an appeal to unity would be in order at these gatherings, where differences in culture and races are often immediately apparent. The hard part, however, is the practical application in a real-world setting. Pan-Chui Lai suggests that one factor that impedes unity is the *approach* that Bible scholars use to do theology. For Chinese theologians, for instance, "Confucianism (especially the tradition of 'xin-xue,' literally speaking, 'heart-mind learning') and Buddhism (especially the Ch'an school) emphasise [sic] the succession of 'heart-mind' over that of 'scripture,' which is only the testimony to the former."[134] This means that when Ephesians 4:3-6 is read—"mak[e] every effort to maintain the unity of the Spirit . . . to the one hope . . . one Lord, one faith, one baptism, one God . . . "—there is no mention of "one scripture." A North American Bible scholar, however, views Scripture as the origin and "yardstick" of faith, so contention between the two cultures is inevitable.[135]

When interpretation is done from a limited view (e.g., European male academic), the range of interpretation in its wake is subject to similarly narrow perspectives. It is true that Scripture is vital to the life of the church and necessary to inform Christian life and community. At the same time, Ephesians 4:3-6 does not make mention of Scripture with regard to what it means to be the church, and unified. Lai proposes reexamination of the "hermeneutic circle" promoted by Luther: "urge Christ against Scripture." That is, theology can "conduct a critique of . . . theological formulations"

---

translated "formed," as in, the form imprinted into the wax of a seal; 2 John 12 χάρτου χάρτης "papyrus sheet," "record," translated "paper." The remaining uses are found in Revelation (13:16, 17; 14:9, 11; 16:2; 19:20; 20:4) as χάραγμα "mark, stamp," translated "mark," as in, "mark of the beast." Still, the "mark" is for life or death in the temporal, as well as the eternal, sense.

134. Lai, "Sino-Theology, the Bible and the Christian Tradition," 276.

135. Ibid. For a practical treatment of doing theology through another cultural lens see Rah, The Next Evangelicalism.

developed throughout history, and can do so with a systematic method. The same process can be applied to culturally diverse theological development.[136] A systematic critique of the theological formulations across historical development, alongside a systematic inquiry into the variety of cultural theological developments, will produce a more comprehensive Christian theology.

Such critiques are one way we grow in unity in the midst of differences. But the question of equipping still remains. How are the saints to be equipped in light of diverse gifts and cultures? The precise meaning of the main verb, to "equip" (καταρτισμός) the saints (4:12), is difficult to nail down.[137] It refers to the verb "gave" (δίδωμι), in verse eleven.[138] And the giver is the one who ascended and descended (v. 9), and the one and only source of the gifts. "He has given one gift to the Church, but this gift manifests itself through different ministries."[139] Juan Manuel Granados Rojas sees the apostles and prophets as bringing together the ministries of the Old Testament and New Testament. Seeing as Rojas sees renders inert the list of five as a hierarchical prescription.[140] The gifts are not listed to inform ecclesial structure and do not indicate that one gift is more important than another. They reflect the grace given to all, equally potent to guide.

The primary role of Paul is to preach the gospel. In this way, for Paul, "the enunciated ministries are related to the ministry of the Word. Apostles, prophets, evangelists, pastors and teachers are all involved in different ways with the same service: preaching the Word."[141] Put another way, all the gifts are involved in different ways with the same service: speaking with God's speech, making room for the (O)other, loving as the Triune God loves.

Love is a prominent theme in Ephesians. Indeed, "*agape* is more important than in . . . any other letter of Paul; it is a primary concern of the letter."[142] Jesus came to fulfill the law and the prophets (Matt 5:17), and

136. England, *Asian Christian Theologies*, 497.

137. Rojas, "Ephesians 4:12," 83–85.

138. Ibid.," 88. Rojas provides a reason for the edit of Psalm 68: "he (Christ) does not receive gifts, but rather gives them to humankind (τοῖς ἀνθρώπις). In such a manner, by means of using the passive voice and modifying the OT quotation the verse stresses the figure of Christ as source of the gift."

139. Ibid., 90.

140. The five gifts listed in Eph 4:11: apostle, prophet, evangelist, pastor, and teacher.

141. Rojas, "Ephesians 4:12," 91. For more on the Eph 4 gifts see Hirsch, *The Forgotten Ways*; and Snyder, *The Problem of Wineskins*.

142. Fuchs, "I Kneel Before the Father and Pray for You," 19.

all who are created through him bear the image of God, with whom Jesus participates. As followers (image-bearers), humankind is made to live through deep prayer, by the leading efficacy of the Spirit, and in increasing union with Christ, so that the community of believers can know and become more like God.

To know God is to have love (1 John 4:7). Christians are known as belonging to Christ by their love for one another. One knows God by loving another; to be known is to be loved and to be loved is to be known (1 John 4:13–16). What is more, "there is no fear in love" (v. 18). The gifts that Paul cites as given to equip, build up the body of Christ, and make mature the church (Eph 4:12–14) have the ultimate concern of accomplishing their roles with love (v. 16). Leaders bear a variety of gifts, all of which have the same goal; one is not greater than another. There is no hierarchical structure, since all are necessary for the task, with "every ligament" promoting growth. And part of this process of growth is being "renewed in the spirit of your minds" (v. 23), mindful of God and each other in order to discern what it means for the body of Christ to exist "according to the likeness of God" (v. 24).

CONCLUSION

God is mindful of us. This God speaks directly to humankind, and imparts glory as the created glorifies God. The distinctions created when the first humans turned a deaf ear to God in the garden no longer shackle. That is, the unique character each person—community, culture, language—possesses that expresses God's image is no longer subject to perversion, control, or misuse because *in Christ* all are free to be who each is, fully and in power. Yet this does not happen individually—the strength lies in unity, and in collaborative, cooperating, love-empowered community. And this begins with the leadership (apostles, prophets, evangelists, shepherds, teachers). Their modeling grows the rest to maturity in the same. All share the same Spirit of the One whom each images. Mindful spiritual practice individually and in the context of a group reflects the image of God who is Triune. When a person engages in the spiritual practice of mindfulness, the same Spirit in each frees the individual from the external power of either controlling another or being controlled due to any distinction. As a result, the group will come to a more creative, collaborative decision as leaders, bringing the church to full maturity, since all the uniquely gifted people will

Biblical and Theological Foundation

be involved and heard as each listens, not turning a deaf ear to the Spirit nor to one another.

Jesus gave up his divinity so that those who would be saved might enter and become more of who they are. Those who enter that space must give it up to each other and again to God who will, in turn, fill them with more of who God is. By giving up his divinity Jesus gave up his power. The incarnation is a summons to Christian leadership to do the same. To make space for another is to relinquish judgment and preconceptions based on the superfluous, the external flesh that was the original object of shame. To give space to one who is different in gender or culture is to allow that space to be filled by another perspective, a broader view, and a fuller understanding of any given task.

Hierarchical power structures are a distortion of the body of Christ. Male and female were created in the image of God for the initial purpose of multiplying and filling the earth. Then, together, the first people shared the responsibility of having dominion over and caring for the earth, and nurturing all it contains. By sharing intimacy and the care for the flourishing of all living things, the first people shared in the knowledge of God and were known by God. This same God is mindful of humankind, and, in response, humankind is mindful of God in the company of one another. Humankind gives glory to God who dwells in and with the people. To give glory is to be attentive (i.e., pay attention) to God in worship—intentionally. It is to be present to God's presence in that moment, with an openness to hear, or notice, God's presence, without harsh judgment, as one is in that moment. To honor another is to similarly make space by being present to each other in that moment, with an openness to hear and notice the unique character of God in the other. This is only possible because humankind was created to give of the self to create life (the side chamber) and can participate in the life of God—know God—through the redemptive work of Christ (the side wound).

The mindfulness practice of prayer deepens the relationship between practitioner and the Spirit of God. In this mindful exchange, it is possible to know the mind of Christ (1 Cor 2). The Christian has the power to discern what is right and good, but only when their prayer is as it "ought" to be (Rom 8:26). That is, the Spirit of God participates in the prayer of those who are indwelled by the same Spirit. This mindful practice of prayer is transformative. By reflecting the character of the *perichoresis*, the Christian leader participates in the relationship of the Persons of the Trinity and becomes *more than*. When leaders practice intentional attentiveness, being open to hear and notice God and each other without judgment, the leadership increases in their capacity to "obtain spiritual direction and understanding." That which previously characterized individuals, often stereotypically associated with difference, is no longer relevant. Difference is transformed by relationship. Christian leadership is then free to "[build] up the body of Christ, until all of us come to the unity of the faith and of the knowledge of the Son of God, to maturity, to the measure of the full stature of Christ" (Eph 4:12–13).

3

Theoretical Grounding

THE PROBLEM

LET US REFOCUS ATTENTION to the problem identified as the aim of this project: the pervasive imposition of stereotypic masculine characteristics expected of leaders that is neither effective nor an accurate understanding of good leadership. It is clear there is a substantial biblical and theological basis to challenge the assumption that stereotypic masculine leadership style is even how we are to lead as God's image-bearers. This chapter will detail the evidence that the fields of anthropology, sociology, biochemistry, etc., reveal to challenge that same assumption. The research shows how these stereotypes may have developed, and the factors that reinforce yet may also be altered for more effective leadership.

THE EVOLUTION OF SOCIAL ROLES

Categories make daily human interaction simpler and efficient. Yet, in chapter 2, it is suggested that categories bring with them acute potential for misuse—chances to dehumanize and mute the unique character that comprises each person. Scripture indicates that each human is unique (e.g., Ps

139:1–24; Jer 29:11–13; Eph 2:10). Other observable influences also attest the countless factors that conspire to generate unique individuals. These include, but are not limited to, personality, physiology, culture, language, family composition, socioeconomic realities, and time in history.[1] The most common general category employed to distinguish humans is gender. It is also one of the most potent and resilient categories, with a long history of its use determining the life course of men and women.

Grounds for using gender to classify an individual's potential, abilities, range of roles, or intellect are based in long-held cultural imperatives. Medical and behavioral scientists are now collaborating with experts in archeology and anthropology to determine the way gender has informed societies' mores and role expectations over time. This is important because culturally derived sex-type expectations influence beliefs concerning an individual's abilities. And these beliefs define the roles assigned by sex-type rather than one's actual ability to perform the role successfully. What is more, roles defined by stereotypic sex-type characteristics limit the range of performance expected—or allowed—for the role. In Christian leadership, it is particularly problematic when the Spirit is quenched (1 Thess 5:19) by those who presume to predetermine how God is moving or how God has gifted others in their midst. The mindfulness practice of group discernment mitigates harsh (pre) judgment and increases openness and awareness of each other, as they are. The result is greater possibility for collaborative decision-making in leadership.

The Anthropology and Archeology of Survival

Social scientists find clues to cultural patterns of behavior in anthropological and archeological data. Earliest human social groups survived by the very act of caring for and protecting each other. Every able member of the group participated in the survival of the community.[2] While some scholars have argued that all human societies are patriarchal,[3] a majority accept

---

1. This range of influence is referred to as the "full-field of formation" by, van Kaam, *Fundamental Formation*.

2. Wood and Eagly, "A Cross-Cultural Analysis of the Behavior of Women and Men," 699–727.

3. See for example, Goldberg, "Why Patriarchy?" 13–21; Rosaldo, "Moral-Analytic Dilemmas Posed by the Intersection of Feminism and Social Science," 76–95; Buss, "The Psychology of Human Mate Selection," in Crawford et al., *Handbook of Evolutionary Psychology*.

the data that show that, for example, pastoral communities were generally communal sharing-style bands with little or insignificant disparity between sexes.[4] Once survival was no longer an imminent threat, and as technology progressed, hierarchies developed that created a culture of dominance. The implications of hierarchical dominance structures are varied. What is important to note for the purposes of this study is that when survival is a major concern, communities generally share the responsibility for that survival, irrespective of age or gender.

One interdisciplinary, cross-cultural analysis of "sex-typed social arrangements" concluded that "sociobiological principles" drive human social groups to designate roles based on sex.[5] The evidence suggests that the majority of personality traits deemed "masculine" or "feminine" are as loosely linked to sex as the clothing or mannerisms of any given time and culture. Size differential, for example, is not a significant factor, since, in evolutionary terms, female to male body-size ratio decreased over time. Females became larger at a greater rate than their male counterparts.[6] So the variance, on average, is not significant to warrant great disparity in role assignment. It is only when an individual's status becomes important in social groupings, social conventions regarding division of labor and perceived (versus actual) ability impose roles for the "efficient" execution of the tasks.

But again, in earliest societies, propriety was not an available luxury if the community was to survive. In gatherer societies across cultures, for instance, women appear to have contributed more to the community than men. In fishing/hunting societies, men had a greater contribution to subsistence (in 1 percent women contributed more).[7] Strength is not a substantial factor in most non-industrialized societies, as usually assumed. For instance, "water fetching is highly strength-intensive, and laundering and fuel gathering also can require substantial strength. Moreover, there is little empirical evidence that characteristically male activities across societies require more strength than characteristically female activities."[8] Division

---

4. Ethnographic studies include Salzman, "Is Inequality Universal?" 31–44; Knauft, "Violence and Sociality in Human Evolution," 391–428.

5. Wood and Eagly, "A Cross-Cultural Analysis of the Behavior of Women and Men," 700.

6. Ibid., 702–703.

7. Ibid., 706.

8. Ibid., 708.

of labor can only be explained by pregnancy and nursing, since carrying an infant on hunting trips is not ideal.

Accordingly, sexual preference pressure is not evidenced as a factor for division of labor in cross-cultural surveys. From the "biosocial perspective, the observed cross-cultural variability in sex-typed behavior is a product of the sexes' reproductive activities and physical attributes in conjunction with the organizational demands of societies and the local environments."[9] When supplemental feeding is available to nursing mothers, they are also free to engage roles available to men. So "patriarchy is not a uniform feature of human societies but instead emerges to the extent that, for example, women's reproductive activities conflict with the behaviors that yield status in a society."[10] That is to say, aside from the reproductive periods of late pregnancy and the nursing of an infant, the anthropological and archeological data indicate leadership roles can be effectively filled by any able adult, irrespective of gender or sex-type.

Shared Leadership to Distributions of Power

A gender-based leadership role is not the sole issue here. It is, in truth, merely a byproduct. The underlying element pertains to a balance of power and hierarchy in leadership. Early nomadic, non-agrarian societies "had foraging economies with few recognizable leadership roles and status differentials among adult men." Displays of dominance were infrequent amid these decentralized groups with "flexible social arrangements." What is more, there is no evidence of status differentiation by sex in these communities, which were "governed in a way that minimized conflict, and [where] intergroup conflict was mild or nonexistent."[11] When communities lived a simple lifestyle and were free from threats from other communities, shared leadership appeared to be compulsory.

In another study that sampled thirty-nine communities, all were egalitarian societies, exhibited "nomadic foraging economies with few recognizable leadership roles and status differentials among adult men," *and* were non-agrarian. Furthermore, there was no evidence of differentiation in status due to sex or age. A shift occured, however, when defense of land became more frequent. While women are represented among the warriors

9. Ibid., 709.
10. Ibid., 704–705.
11. Ibid., 710.

Theoretical Grounding

throughout history and across cultures, the span of time necessary to nurse an infant is sufficient to socialize women to a lower status. In addition, the larger size and musculature of the upper male body, while superficial, compounded by the inefficiency of *nursing* mothers engaging in war, promoted the socialization of male power over females. This intensified in the case of warfare and the need to support the force engaging in war. "Societies that engage in very frequent warfare are particularly marked by gender inequality."[12]

When technology evolved to increase production and ease labor, strength was no longer a valid factor regarding a person's ability to contribute to subsistence (e.g., income). The introduction of farming tools and innovation in irrigation, for example, made strength and size irrelevant to role fitness. Across cultures, even in childcare, mothers of infants are rarely sole caregivers (this was true in only about 25 percent of societies analyzed), and by the time the child is weaned, they are in the care of the mother less than 50 percent of the time. A majority of cultures divide tasks between sexes, but "the majority of tasks [are] not uniquely associated with one sex."[13] Put another way, most cultures throughout history assign specific roles to either gender, but the expectations are seldom the same and are rarely related to sex-type.

Essentially, "as technologies such as irrigation developed and societies enlarged, human-environmental relations also moved away from egalitarian and reciprocal partnerships with other species and ecosystems to more directive interactions."[14] The connotations of cultural symbols evolved over time. For example, at one time water, necessary for life, represented the feminine, the female deity. Once tools were developed to assist agrarian societies with irrigation, water came to indicate masculine power. Because irrigation made the control of water possible, water could then be understood as property and conscribed to the property rights according to hierarchical power. No longer a collective source of renewal, water became an economic asset.

What developed over time is what one anthropologist describes as "the doctrine of universal sexual asymmetry . . . [and it] has achieved the status of theoretical as well as political hegemony in Western thought. This assumption has resulted in the naturalization of male-centered

---

12. Ibid., 713.
13. Ibid., 707.
14. Strang, "Lording It Over the Goddess," 86.

reconstructions of the past that have dominated archaeology for more than two centuries."[15] Differences are "typically arranged hierarchically," setting up a system that makes necessary the dominance of one type over another, and are applied to sex as well as race, ethnicity, and vocation.[16] But this does not need to be an inevitable trajectory. In the case of *contemporary* foragers, "the virtual elimination of alpha-male behavior is possible because ... political coalitions are able to act efficiently on a moral basis, with a conscience-based sense of right and wrong as a political catalyst that intensifies negative group reactions against personal self-aggrandizement."[17] That is to say, when the community assigns negative connotations to self-promotion, the leadership acts on a moral imperative to cooperate and work toward the good of the whole. Cooperative behavior and consensus style leadership act as a moral barometer to disable sedition and perpetuate further cooperation.

Idealized Leadership Across Cultures

Behaviors are adaptations to social negotiations, and these social negotiations are what make up a culture and cultural norms. Social groupings for the sake of survival are common in the animal kingdom, and mimicry is a means to communicate to younger members how to survive and thrive in the community. What is uniquely human is the explicit use of teaching.[18] Teaching assumes that what is to be learned is not instinctual, per se; rather, the instruction provides the reasoning behind the behaviors, based on agreed-upon sets of mores. The terms of survival are revised when new technologies develop that affect, in turn, the conditions for leadership. For instance, what is considered an ideal leadership system of checks-and-balance in the United States government is in practice less about merit and qualifications suited to a specific job than it is about the ability to control and maintain that control.[19] While the Western idolization of autonomy increases the likelihood of creative output, the system is left open to corruption. Group discernment in leadership, on the other hand, welcomes

---

15. Marler, "The Myth of Universal Patriarchy," 168.
16. Ibid., 169.
17. Boehm, "Ancestral Hierarchy and Conflict," 845.
18. Schaller, *Evolution, Culture, and the Human Mind*, 15.
19. Fukuyama, "What Is Governance?" 348.

the uniquely creative contribution of the individual while trusting the corporate mindfulness practice to bring consensus to the problem at hand.

The move to hierarchical leadership was further reinforced when monotheism was introduced, and a number of cultural shifts occurred that become more pronounced by European Christianity. One change that accompanied "monotheism and 'enlightened' rationality was a shift toward individuated forms of resource ownership, which required commensurately individual constructions of social identity."[20] That is, land and property became the coin, and ownership conferred power. The Judeo-Christian ethic promotes the sharing of property, but cultural and economic imperatives dominated society and blurred the line with religious practice. From the 1500s, the "hegemonic colonial enterprises" reinforced culture over nature. Cultural anthropologist Veronica Strang observes:

> There were earlier efforts to impose religious changes on conquered peoples (this being a feature of most colonial invasions), as well as upsurges of conflict between the major monotheistic religions, for example, in the Crusades. But the technology that enabled major oceanic voyages and produced massive disparity in military strength permitted far more ambitious colonial enterprises.[21]

The imposition of culture-bound aspects of religion made the message of freedom in Christ and God's supreme love contingent on the acceptance of the forms practiced by the colonizing societies.

In addition, as agricultural economies developed, clans propagated societies and splintered the family unit. Gendered roles became more pronounced as "public" and "domestic" spheres emerged as further demarcated. Female care for infants relegated a woman's contribution to the society to the private sphere, limiting her range of influence. Another effect of the introduction of irrigation systems was a demotion of the spiritual character of the elements. So when the spiritual component of interaction with the elements shifted, "a more empowered and human-focused relationship with the material world and its other inhabitants emerged."[22] Though veneration of elemental spirits continued, there were shifts in form, from animistic to "gendered persona." The symbols of the spiritual life of communities reflect

---

20. Strang, "Lording It Over the Goddess," 103.
21. Ibid., 76.
22. Ibid., 93.

the societal structure, and objectification of the female form became the most sinister example of that.[23]

Later, the Enlightenment era birthed scientific inquiry. Classification is a prominent feature of this pattern of thought and played a strong role in separating nature from humankind. The environment became "other" in scientific terms (versus sacred). Classifying objectifies, and making a class an object implies ownership over the object, with attendant power and dominance. The difference in class is found in the space between those who "dwell 'within the sphere' of their surroundings and those for whom the earth is a 'globe' to be acted upon."[24] The restricted class, or space, is the inverse of the *Shekinah* discussed in chapter two, where broad space is given, filled, and given back. It is an exchange of one religious meaning for another: re-creative water is now "ordained" to civilize the ignorant, and the predestined manager replaces presence and being present to one another. Émile Durkheim plainly grasped that "religious cosmologies [mirror] sociopolitical arrangements" and the acquisition of scientific knowledge.[25] It is in this way that humankind makes gods in the image of humankind.

By spiritualizing the elements that humans can manage and manipulate, religious sentiment infuses the language of leadership and gives a "divine authority" to its decrees. Ideal leadership is then only "cross-cultural" insofar as colonizing and dominating agents impose their own ideals on other cultures. The current political situation in the United States, for instance, acts to maintain class distinctions but is wrapped in religious language. Individuals and communities who linger in poverty, for multifarious reasons, do not have the same access to possibilities. Additionally, those in the urban pockets of greater poverty are overrepresented by discrete groups of minorities. These dynamics shape the way children grow up understanding their potential (or lack), and the power-disparity is perpetuated.[26] While addressing the complex and copious factors that make leadership available to some rather than others is beyond the scope of this thesis, mindfulness practice in shared leadership groups is a start toward making things right

---

23. The evolution of the objectification of the female form has relevance to this thesis, but further exploration of the implications, not the least of which is the scourge of pornography, is beyond its scope.

24. Strang, "Lording It Over the Goddess," 105.

25. Ibid., 106.

26. Heberle and Carter, "Cognitive Aspects of Young Children's Experience of Economic Disadvantage," 723–46.

for the underserviced.[27] Doing so in the context of church leadership is a further step to redeem the nefarious effects the religious-political connection currently perpetuates.

Evolutionary Biology: Sharing and Dominance

A significant limitation to *sociological* inquiries involves the psychometrics used to identify gender distinctions, in particular, and what constitutes maturity within gender constructs. Most measures are ill-equipped to address cross-cultural facets of gender roles. And in fact, nearly all cross-cultural studies are, in practice, biculture surveys comparing North American with East Asian identities.[28] Several major studies conducted over the last two decades are beginning to change perceptions and methodology in this area, asking different kinds of questions to understand how culture informs gender roles and leadership practice. The process of analysis and the justifications behind systems of role assignments are enormously complex. Still, the general consensus is that if the community demands a set of behaviors, the residents will conform. And while sex-type role is the primary focus here, the implications are transferrable to stereotypic ethnic-type role assignments, among other types of marginalization. It is likely no coincidence that emancipation of black slaves and American women's suffrage unfolded in virtual simultaneity.[29]

In a recent study conducted in the greater Sydney, Australia, area, the men were of a variety of ethnicities, ages, and socioeconomic standings. Still, the majority of men maintained an overarching common assent to "patriarchal ideologies" and an "idealized Western patriarchal masculinity."[30] On the other hand, in the Semai and Waorani tribes, gender roles are not differentiated. The Semai of Malaysia enjoy a "homogenous, egalitarian, intimate and peaceful society" where violence is absent—though they are fierce warriors when called to defend themselves. The Waorani of Ecuador

---

27. More on the effects of mindfulness practice and shared leadership is developed and explained below.

28. Becker et al., "Culture and the Distinctiveness Motive," 387.

29. The Emancipation Proclamation was signed by Abraham Lincoln in 1863. U.S. National Archives & Records Administration, "The Emancipation Proclamation." The American women's suffrage movement was established in 1867. International Alliance of Women, "International Alliance of Women for Suffrage and Legal Citizenship."

30. Bettman, "Patriarchy," 23.

kill and feud, but husbands do not exercise violence against their wives, and they immediately ceased participation in violence when they embraced Christianity. Both the Semai and Waorani communities exemplify the power of discourse over violence in the face of limitless capacity for the same.[31]

Ascribing specific characteristics to gender as a means for dominance can be observed in political structures of other relatively recent societies. A post-hoc study of ethnographies analyzing features of late twentieth-century east African warfare trends between state and non-state societies determined that "state societies commit atrocities during warfare significantly more than nonstate societies."[32] Furthermore, "when torture is practiced, state societies are significantly more likely than non-state societies to torture noncombatants."[33] Reasons for coercive methods by state societies are complex. But states do tend to be more autocratic and led by authoritarian governments. Such governments use more coercive methods to control the people, so it follows that similar behavior will be seen in warfare. In addition, multiplex societies are generally less nurturing to their children and more severe in overall socialization, making fear-tactics more likely in the chaos of war. In non-state societies, individuals rely more on extended and non-family networks that foster a cooperative sense of obligation to others.

From a biological perspective, there is a type of feedback loop that occurs between hormone levels and environmental influences. Increased androgen, for example, seems to increase dominance behavior and the likelihood of securing dominant positions.[34] Dominant positions reinforce the production of (and consequent increase in) androgen. The higher level "reduces trust, increases risk-taking accompanied by increased sensitivity to rewards and reduced sensitivity to punishment, and also facilitates resource acquisition and high status via [consent]."[35] Additionally, cortisol levels increase in defeat scenarios. And the pattern of hormone responses is the same in men *and* women.[36] Disrupting the cycle can do the oppo-

---

31. Ibid., 24.

32. Ember et al., "Risk, Uncertainty, and Violence in Eastern Africa," 49.

33. Ibid., 50.

34. Oliveira and Oliveira, "Androgen Modulation of Social Decision Making Mechanisms in the Brain," 2.

35. Ibid., 3.

36. Jiménez et al., "Effects of Victory and Defeat on Testosterone and Cortisol

site: when experiencing a decrease in social status, dominance-inciting hormones circulate at a reduced rate.[37] That is to say, dominance by the individual with higher levels of androgen coursing throughout the system is not inevitable. Nor does the evidence suggest that it is "natural" for those with higher levels of androgen to be in dominant positions.

The point is not gender politics or an exchange of power from one entity to another, based on revenge that stems from disenfranchisement. The point is to effect "transformation and the retrieval of inner authority that systems of domination externalize."[38] Hierarchical systems imply graded levels of power reinforced by external controls. Nonconformity must be punished for the maintenance of order and the status quo. External controls bypass the inner motivations that would facilitate collaboration and greater creative effort. Group discernment, on the other hand, allows the space to draw from the personal inner authorities and the disposition of openness to the *other*. When leadership is shared, violence is far less likely and cooperation probable.

Acts of violence and violence acted upon another impact the biology of both people. Hormone and chemical activity do influence brain activation and structure. Brain activity elicits a bodily, behavioral response that interacts with the environment (e.g., a social setting). The environment, in turn, reinforces the behavior, whereby hormone-brain activity is augmented. Because of this, adaptive behavior cannot be considered apart from the complex mechanisms that influence the organism (e.g., a person). More about these systems will be examined below. It is enough for now to say that the socio-evolutionary development of leadership within a social setting is influenced by exceedingly complex systems and factors. Ascribing sex-type to a particular role does not need to be contingent upon strictly "natural" composition or fitness. Indeed, cooperative group leadership irrespective of gender secured the most ideal outcomes when it mattered most (survival).[39] Evolutionary theory does not adequately explain how cooperation can be normative, since fitness did not deselect for mechanisms producing, for instance, elevated levels of androgen.[40] Intentional behavioral patterns

---

Response to Competition," from the abstract.

37. Oliveira and Oliveira, "Androgen Modulation of Social Decision Making Mechanisms in the Brain," 2.
38. Marler, "The Myth of Universal Patriarchy," 181.
39. Apicella et al., "Social Networks and Cooperation in Hunter-Gatherers," 497–501.
40. Evolutionary theory states that unnecessary biological features do not survive

change hormonal levels but do not alter, necessarily, the mechanisms that can reverse the change.[41] Something *more than* factors into the equation. This *factor* speaks to the strength and range of influence on brain chemistry, as well as on the structure of a community.

Leadership that has been traditionally dominated by the male sex, and values stereotypic masculine traits is, to an increasing extent, seen as stunted. The contemporary evolution of the expansion of women in leadership roles makes perceiving the impact that much more palpable. It is not that stereotypic feminine traits are seen as a more effective leadership style. In fact, women who are "allowed" into leadership roles lead, for the most part, in a stereotypic masculine manner. Rather, it is that women are traditionally socialized to adopt feminine style traits and roles, so they often integrate those characteristics into their leadership. In this way, researchers are now finding that most effective leadership and teaching styles incorporate both types of characteristics, and that androgynous features are most successful.[42] The following sections will outline how mindfulness attention and practices engender the conditions for androgynous expression in leadership—at least, sensitivity to and identification with the needs of the student or those being led.[43] The importance of this focus is made manifest by the expanding globalization (recall the phenomenon of glocalization illustrated chapter two) as well as evidence that maintains the error of ascribing sex-type to certain roles,[44] and to the role of leadership in particular.

MINDFULNESS RESEARCH

The pervasiveness of mindfulness research in the fields of neuroscience, clinical medicine, and psychology is evidenced by the number of published studies in peer-reviewed journals. The National Institute of Health alone

---

generations, so societies that are more cooperative should no longer express elevated levels of androgen. However, androgen continues to be produced by an individual's endocrine system in even the most docile of societies.

41. Nowak and Coakley, *Evolution, Games, and God*, 151–97.

42. Kent and Moss, "Effects of Sex and Gender Role on Leader Emergence," 1337; Wheeless and Potorti, "Student Assessment of Teacher Masculinity and Femininity," 259–62.

43. Jensen, *Teaching with the Brain in Mind*. See especially chapter 12, "Schools with the Brain in Mind," particularly section 2, "Supporting Good Instruction and Good Instructors: Change with the Brain in Mind."

44. Tran, "Narrating Lives, Narrating Faith," 189.

reported in 2010 that, in the preceding five years, it had funded more than 150 studies about the application of mindfulness.[45] And the number of publications on the subject of mindfulness efficacy rose from 80 in 1990 to over 600 in 2006.[46] The volume of analyses is enough to grab the attention of leaders in any field. That mindfulness practice is echoed in biblical narratives and instruction suggests its relevance for Christian leadership training as well.

Definition of Mindfulness

Mindfulness-Based Stress Reduction (MBSR) was first developed by Kabat-Zinn in the 1970s to assist his cancer patients with pain management. It has since proved effective for psychological pain and distress as well.[47] As a reminder, for our proposes here, mindfulness will be defined as an awareness that arises out of the mode of being by paying kind attention, on purpose, in the current moment, without harsh judgment, to things as they are.[48] It is a present-moment disposition of curiosity and openness to the Spirit "bearing witness with our spirit that we are children of God" (Rom 8:16).

By *without judgment*, Kabat-Zinn suggests "think[ing] of it as an invitation to suspend judging as much as we can and just be aware of what is unfolding from moment to moment." As opposed to judging something as good or bad, it is "discernment . . . the kind of operation of wisdom where you can see the subtleties—the thousand shades of grey between black and white . . . which is absolutely essential to and part and parcel of the cultivation of mindfulness."[49]

---

45. Williams and Kabat-Zinn, "Mindfulness," 3.

46. Goldberg et al., "The Role of Therapeutic Alliance in Mindfulness Interventions," 936.

47. For an extensive review of the mindfulness research, see Hart et al., "Mind the Gap in Mindfulness Research," 453–66.

48. Kabat-Zinn developed the basic definition as a result of his research on pain management for cancer patients in the 1970s. Kabat-Zinn, "Mindfulness-Based Interventions in Medicine and Psychiatry," in Andy Fraser, *The Healing Power of Meditation*. See also Hart et al., "Mind the Gap in Mindfulness Research," 453–66; Robins et al., "Effects of Mindfulness-Based Stress Reduction on Emotional Experience and Expression," 117–31.

49. Shonin, "This Is Not Mindfulness by Any Stretch of the Imagination," §3.

Effects of Mindfulness

Mindfulness practice is shown variously to alleviate the perception of physical pain associated with cancer treatment and the psychological pain of loss and trauma, and to prevent the acute Post Traumatic Stress Disorder (PTSD) response to combat in military professionals. Practices may include awareness of breathing, walking meditation, mindful speaking, and listening. At the same time, long-term effects are seen more prominently when the practice is approached as more than merely a technique, but when there is meaning derived from or motivating its use.

A study of Australian law students revealed that when law students were given information and instruction concerning the benefits to mental health, including mindfulness practices, the students were more likely to choose these activities. The researchers found that by "improving the awareness of significant findings in psychological science, ... [students took] notice [of] risk factors in themselves."[50] Indeed, even an elementary grasp of neural processes provides a tool with which even the perception of one's situation might be changed. Introducing mindfulness practices that help law students understand the mechanisms that promote mental health and well-being creates an environment in which mental stress is recognized for what it is (i.e., without judgment, as things are). Judson A. Brewer et al., explain:

> Affective bias underlies emotional distortions of attention and memory, preventing individuals from accurately assessing what is happening in the present moment and acting accordingly. Mindfulness functions to decouple pleasant and unpleasant experience from habitual reactions of craving and aversion, by removing the affective bias that fuels such emotional reactivity. It is the absence of emotional distortions, we suggest, that allows mindfulness practitioners to "see things as they are."[51]

For the law students, understanding the science supporting mindfulness practice was enough to produce noticeable changes in thought and behavior.

---

50. Colin James, "Law Student Wellbeing," 217–33.
51. Brewer et al., "Craving to Quit," 74–75.

Theoretical Grounding

Altruism: Living Simply and Socially Conscious

A major component of mindfulness is the practice of attention to thoughts and sensations experienced from moment to moment. The skill developed by this practice is the self-regulation of thoughts and reactions that lead to openness and nonjudgment as feelings arise. It is at once awareness of and orientation toward the experience, as well as reflection on the experience with a sort of detachment referred to as *re-perceiving* or *cognitive decentering*.[52] This reflective detachment is also found in the teaching of St. Ignatius of Loyola and described as "holy indifference." This disposition is shown to lead to the practical feature of orienting oneself to both a simple lifestyle and a consciousness of germane issues that impact the community. In other words, mindfulness yields altruism.

Tania Singer et al., describes altruism in this way: "*Prosocial behavior*, or *altruism*, is . . . defined as costly acts that increase another person's benefits."[53] The New Oxford American Dictionary defines altruism as "the belief in or practice of disinterested and selfless concern for the well-being of others."[54] It is this sense of "disinterest" that describes "holy indifference" or nonjudgement. It is a disposition of concern for another that is not based on a personal need for praise or reciprocation. Neither is it concerned about whether the subject of the altruistic presence and/or act is open to receiving or even hostile to succor. Altruism as a result of mindfulness practice can step outside the self to notice—and understand—the need or pain of another. In this way, it is good for the health of the community and for the preservation of humanity.

Drawing from Darwin's "social selection" model, Christopher Boehm investigates the evolution of altruism. Specifically, Boehm sees a "genetic selection that is accomplished by the social, as opposed to the natural environment."[55] If one has a reputation for helping, others will be more likely to help that person. Such a person is also more attractive as a partner or mate, and they will prove stronger together, as mutually helpful, which strengthens the community.[56] Reciprocal altruism acts as glue and magnet,

---

52. Hülsheger et al., "The Power of Presence," 1115.

53. Singer et al., "Effects of Oxytocin and Prosocial Behavior on Brain Responses," 782.

54. *New Oxford American Dictionary*.

55. Boehm, "The Moral Consequences of Social Selection," 168.no. 2/3 (2014

56. Ibid., 169. For an example of the strength of social selection in the development of early Christianity, see Stark, *The Rise of Christianity*.

attracting others to the mutually beneficial community. "Evolutionary conscience" supports adherence to group rules, functions out of a particular brain region (prefrontal cortex), and depends on empathy (paralimbic system) to evolve. "While these brain areas and many of the associated functions are far from unique to humans, responses like blushing socially, feeling shame, and morally internalizing group values such as those which favor generosity seem to be ours alone."[57]

Correspondingly, and noted above, in early mobile communities (Late Pleistocene), social hierarchies are nearly non-detectible, as cooperation was necessary for survival. At the same time, effective cooperation needs a moralistic "political egalitarianism . . . [with a] heavily neutralized alpha power." It was these conditions that made the sharing of "coveted large game on an equalized basis" possible for hunting communities.[58] Indeed, "hunting could only be efficient for an entire band if dominant individuals who wanted to use their power to control and basically over-consume meat were curbed."[59] The typical antelope is small enough to require "fair," modest portions, which an "alpha-male" would not likely disperse.

Even more, though, due to the distinctly human shame reaction of blushing and a fear of group disappointment (i.e., conscience), domination was, in general, not necessary to get the community to adhere to group mores. What developed, then, were "normative rules" that "heavily favored generosity, honesty and humility."[60] The promotion of generosity as a rule would not be necessary if it were not a characteristic of being human. Group social control functions to protect the community from the selfish predator. Generous people are at greater risk "unless they can consolidate their interests, band together actively, and insist aggressively on keeping their moral communities cooperative, egalitarian, and relatively free of social predation."[61] Humans generally prefer dealings with trustworthy people. For egalitarian hunting bands, as for any egalitarian community, humility is a necessary component for overriding bullying. Shame, or "social pain" (versus capital punishment), then, "allow[s] for reform, and possessing

---

57. Ibid.
58. Ibid., 171.
59. Ibid., 175–176.P
60. Ibid., 177.
61. Boehm, "The Moral Consequences of Social Selection," 178.></EndNote>

an efficient evolutionary conscience makes such reform possible through *self-control*."[62]

Altruism is a social feature that has biological markers in brain structure and sets humans apart from animals. It characterizes humanity and must be cultivated for the survival of the community. What is more,

> Moralistic group sanctioning is so predictable and so collectivized that it may well be the most basic kind of human cooperation we experience outside the family. In spite of the various ancestral precursors, the powerful type of social selection that results is distinctly human, and it has resulted in brain functions and states of feeling that are sufficiently unique that they set us apart as moral beings.[63]

Moralistic group sanctioning works because a group of people is mindful of how others are related to each other and themselves. Collective morality is generally the purview of social science. More specific, the field of social mindfulness began as social activism, but as it is described in social psychology the focus goes one step further: attention to unmasking meaning. Based on Erik Erikson's schematic of the hierarchy of needs, the premise is that the ultimate human endeavor is not for power or pleasure, but "the search for meaning."[64] When the motivation for external power or internal, selfish pleasure is circumvented by deference to the community, group mindfulness practices are successful in eliciting a sense of meaning. And, "when participating with others in a mindfulness session, we are involved in a social context that affords the opportunity to reflect upon our own thoughts and experiences and exchange these with the others."[65] It is a freedom to accept self *and* regard the situation of another. It is a distinctly human way to make sense of things and to service something outside, *more than* oneself.[66]

---

62. Ibid., 179, emphasis mine.

63. Ibid., 179–180.

64. Nilsson, "A Four-Dimensional Model of Mindfulness and Its Implications for Health," 164.

65. Ibid., 165.

66. Wong, "Meaning Therapy," 155.

Memory, Creativity, and Addiction Recovery

Memory is another element improved by mindfulness practice. The twentieth-century Spanish filmmaker Luis Buñuel observed this about memory: "You have to begin to lose your memory, if only in bits and pieces, to realize that memory is what makes our lives. Life without memory is no life at all . . . our memory is our coherence, our reason, our feeling, even our action. Without it, we are nothing. . . ."[67] With an increasing life span and burgeoning retirement-aged population, the topic of memory loss is of considerable import. Several studies that researched the effects of mindfulness practice on memory retention show great promise.[68] Related research reveals the effects of mindfulness techniques on creativity and the ability to make creative connections, which have played a significant role in more effective addiction recovery. These areas are researched separately, and from a variety of disciplines, but they still reveal the mutual, cumulative effect that emphasizing one area has on the improvement in another. The mutuality of effect highlights the necessity of maintaining a holistic approach to mindfulness training.

The Jungian psychologist Henry Corbin introduced the term *mundus imaginalis* to describe the cognitive function of "imaginative power" as an "interpretive lens, a way of knowing 'reality.'"[69] Imagination is also an effective means by which cultural anthropologists and archeologists may reconstruct a past culture. Norvene Vest views this approach as a "recovery of soul," a way to discern the life of past cultures "releasing hidden meanings through imaginative reconstruction of the sacred."[70] The approach can be correlated to the ancient Christian practice of *lectio divina*, or "divine reading" of Scripture with meditation and prayer. *Lectio divina* and imaginative prayer invite individuals and groups into this very act of imaginative reconstruction of the sacred.[71] Time in reflection, listening, imagining makes room—space—for discernment and the understanding of past cultures, as well as the latent substance behind the ancient Scriptures. It is a sort of memory imprinted by the Spirit bearing witness to the spirits of human creation (Rom 8:16).

---

67. Buñuel, *My Last Breath*, 4–5.
68. See for example, Gino and Desai, "Memory Lane and Morality," 743–58.
69. Vest, "Is Reverie to Be Trusted?" 240–241.
70. Ibid., 241.
71. See for example, Oestreicher and Warner, *Imaginative Prayer for Youth Ministry*.

Theoretical Grounding

Marija Gimbutas, a Lithuanian archeologist, studied Neolithic and Bronze-Age, European cultures. She spent decades musing over photographs and line drawings of figurines that depict a "well-developed" ancient culture with cultic traditions of art and architecture.[72] Gimbutas posited that these artifacts—images of culture—act as language that can tell of its structure, a "meta-language."[73] While much of Gimbutas's focus concentrated on explaining the prevalence of female deities, she ultimately came to these conclusions: (1) "the sacred is inseparable from all the actions and relationships of daily life," and (2) "the goddess is not merely a sex symbol, but is symbolic of 'the mystery of birth and death and the renewal of life. . . .'"[74] Imagination assumes something *more than*, something *other*; it asks that one step outside the self and consider another perspective or vantage.

It is this aspect of acknowledging an Other that set apart the 12-Step Program, Alcoholics Anonymous (AA), from other strictly behavioral addiction recovery interventions. AA has the additional feature of operating from the context of group support. What is missing, however, are the mindfulness practices that invite participants to face pain and discomfort for what it is—the practices that free the person to experience the pain so as to move through it and beyond.[75] Research psychologists found statistically significant increases in addict resilience when a Mindfulness Based Relapse Prevention (MBRP) program was utilized.[76] The ability to detach emotion from pain or craving increases the ability to reframe the underlying stress precipitating the addictive behavior.[77] In smoking cessation interventions, mindfulness training is shown to be effective in lowering the heart rate, which reduces relapses[78] and cravings.[79] Also, evidence for mindfulness training's efficacy to separate unpleasant sensations from negative emotion

---

72. Vest, "Is Reverie to Be Trusted?," 243.

73. Ibid.

74. Ibid., 244.

75. It must be noted that a fair majority of AA programs are increasingly incorporating mindfulness practices in their group meetings. And the perspective that allows one to encounter compassion toward self and then direct it back again to another is integrated into the 12-Step Program.

76. Daneshjoo et al., "Comparing Effectiveness of Schema Therapy and Mindfulness-Based Relapse Prevention (MBRP)," 577.

77. Brewer et al., "Craving to Quit," 75.

78. Libby et al., "Meditation-Induced Changes in High-Frequency Heart Rate Variability Predict Smoking Outcomes," 6.

79. Elwafi et al., "Mindfulness Training for Smoking Cessation," 222–29.

is increasingly accessible.[80] Thus, mindfulness practices influence decision-making, enabling decisions to be made in response to things as they actually are.[81]

Mindfulness training and practice reorient the practitioner to see things as they are by designating time and space to reflection, which creates freedom to imagine and reimagine. This very act reduces impulsive reactions that characterize harmful addictions as well as unconsidered prejudices. The mindful person is apt to express altruism and, consequently, be more cooperative, and able to apprehend the true issues at hand. Moreover, the aspect of the brain that services memory is improved by mindfulness practice, making space—an openness—for creative options beyond the self (i.e., the Spirit) to overcome addiction or make cooperative decisions.

The Biochemical and Neurological Evidence

Behavioral markers and social cues are valid indicators of the effects of behavioral changes such as introducing a routine of mindfulness practice, but they are incomplete. Medical technology can now be used to measure brain chemistry and activity, as well as blood pressure and heart performance. This is another way mindfulness practice can be measured in terms of its effects on the brain and body. In the hands of professionals, neuroimaging can show, for instance, how "regular [mindfulness] training has a positive effect on the prefrontal cortex (PFC) and anterior cingulum (ACC), which, among other things, are significantly involved in the regulation of emotion and stress."[82] Studies of physiological markers related to the sympathetic (SNS) and parasympathetic (PNS) branches of the autonomic nervous system (ANS) also show better coping under stressful conditions as a result of mindfulness training.

Cortisol is the hormone produced by the adrenal gland and released as a result of anxiety. Anxiety, in turn, primes the body to experience pain.[83]

---

80. Amaro, "Thinking: I," 189–92; Witkiewitz and Bowen, "Depression, Craving, and Substance Use Following a Randomized Trial of Mindfulness-Based Relapse Prevention," 362–74; Witkiewitz et al., "Mindfulness-Based Relapse Prevention for Substance Craving," 1563–71.

81. EnginDeniz et al., "The Prediction of Decision Self Esteem and Decision Making Styles by Mindfulness," 45–50.

82. Nilsson, "A Four-Dimensional Model of Mindfulness and Its Implications for Health," 170.

83. Burch and Penman, *You Are Not Your Pain*, 19.

The experience confuses the brain and can begin the cycle of "misattribution of arousal." This occurs when emotions are misattributed to pain, and, in turn, triggered by pain, particularly if the cycle is chronic.[84] Elissa Epel et al., explains: "Psychological stress cognitions, particularly appraisals of threat and ruminative thoughts, can lead to prolonged states of reactivity. In contrast, mindfulness meditation techniques appear to shift cognitive appraisals from threat to challenge, decrease ruminative thought, and reduce stress arousal."[85] The telomere, the protective sheath at the tips of DNA strands that fray over time, is also negatively impacted by cortisol, and mindfulness training is shown to "have salutary effects on telomere length by reducing cognitive stress and stress arousal and increasing positive states of mind and hormonal factors that may promote telomere maintenance."[86] Intact telomeres mean a longer, healthier life.

Beyond a healthy lifestyle, mindful disposition resulted in greater physical health in a study of college women, and "better physical health was related to better sleep quality and healthier eating patterns as well as higher levels of *dispositional* mindfulness."[87] In another analysis, when given "tolcapone, a drug that prolongs the effects of dopamine, a brain chemical associated with reward and motivation in the prefrontal cortex," research participants were significantly more egalitarian. They "were more sensitive to and less tolerant of social inequity, the perceived relative economic gap between a study participant and a stranger."[88] In other words, the brain chemistry and neuronal activity that mindfulness training generates manifests itself in behavior such as cooperative egalitarian dispositions and awareness of the poverty dilemma.

The Developing Brain Structure

The biochemical reaction in a brain engaged in mindfulness practice is the same as a nursing mother bonding with her newborn. It is well documented that mindfulness contemplation increases the hormones that elicit a sense

---

84. Ibid., 67.
85. Epel et al., "Can Meditation Slow Rate of Cellular Aging?" in Bushell et al, *Longevity, Regeneration, and Optimal Health*, from the abstract.
86. Ibid.
87. Murphy et al., "The Benefits of Dispositional Mindfulness in Physical Health," 344, emphasis mine.
88. Sáez et al., "Dopamine Modulates Egalitarian Behavior in Humans," 912.

of well-being. Oxytocin, in particular, is strongly associated with modulating social behavior to "reduce endocrine and psychological responses to social stress ... and to increase trust, generosity, and the ability to infer the mental states of another person ('mind reading')."[89] Evidence for well-being can now also be observed in the structure of the brain. For instance, the amygdala is central to the brain's alarm system and uses two-thirds of its neurons to process negative emotion. Yet the hormones involved in negative emotions (cortisol, epinephrine, etc.) are comparatively stronger and more urgent than hormones that signal well-being (oxytocin, etc.).[90] One study demonstrated that selfish people show high activation in the amygdala, indicating greater stress and fear of threats (specifically of personal pain).[91] Still, even an elementary grasp of neural processes is enough to alter the perception of one's situation and neural structure when that awareness is part of the Mindfulness training focus.

The adolescent brain is particularly impressionable. The fatty myelin that insulates neuronal connections (synapses) is not fully developed until the mid-to-late twenties, and it develops from the back of the brain to the front. So the areas that manage impulse control and reasoned reflection (prefrontal lobe/cortex, near the front of the brain) are the last to make fully developed connections (insulation). Stress changes the chemistry and environment of the brain, increasing the risk that adolescents will suffer depression as adults. What is more, mental state is dependent on the maturity of the brain. Depression manifests in this last-developed prefrontal lobe. So when exceptionally high levels of stress hormones etch the structure of the developing brain, the risk for adulthood depression is especially high.

Additionally, alcohol is more toxic to the developing brain, counteracting the effects of learning and affecting memory. And with more open synaptic cells available in the adolescent brain, there are also more opportunities for drugs like marijuana to "lock on" and inhibit memory and learning. Moreover, messages taught regarding abilities and gifts etch pathways alongside these other factors and can have lasting effects on future decisions. Since, for instance, "studies involving cognitive tasks do not

---

89. Singer et al., "Effects of Oxytocin and Prosocial Behavior on Brain Responses to Direct and Vicariously Experienced Pain," 782.

90. Burch and Penman, *You Are Not Your Pain*, 139–141.

91. Singer et al., "Effects of Oxytocin and Prosocial Behavior on Brain Responses to Direct and Vicariously Experienced Pain," 789.

Theoretical Grounding

show gender-based increases or decreases,"[92] approaches to education are exceedingly important.[93] Mindfulness training with adolescents is shown to lower markers of stress and to decrease risky behavior (e.g., unprotected sex, drug use, aggressive driving, etc.).[94] The educational system is one venue for mindfulness training, but a consistent, relationship-centered setting is indispensable for helping young people cultivate healthy brain development. In addition, parenting strategies and relationships are not only a useful means of mindfulness training; they also play a role in the mindfulness *process*.

It is important to understand the development of the young person's brain and the factors that impact that development. A mindfulness disposition plays a major role in the health of the brain and, still more, the developing brain. Christian leadership is in a unique position to influence not only the groups it leads firsthand, but also the families who are involved in that context (e.g., a congregation). Mindfulness is cultivated in private isolation, *and* it is further nurtured and maintained in a collective milieu. With mobile devices in the hands of an increasing number of young people—at younger and younger ages—distraction and physical disconnection are a mounting problem. Leading in a manner that reflects a mindfulness disposition is an effective way to address this situation.

GROUP MINDFULNESS: DISCERNMENT

The North American church has typically treated church structure as if it were a business, with the leadership governed by a CEO and a corporate hierarchy.[95] The argument is that the church functions in the "real world" and must accommodate accordingly. But organizations that consider "real world" leadership as a "predesigned bureaucracy governed by policies and laws, where people are expected to do what they're told and wait for instructions," function under a "dangerous fiction that destroys our capac-

---

92. Jensen and Nutt, *The Teenage Brain*, 229.

93. Changes in approaches to gender-based instruction have changed test outcomes (and the very structure of the brain) between the early 1990s and 2015. The earlier time saw no difference in math scores between boys and girls, but boys significantly outscored girls by high school. Today, there is no difference in math scores between genders. Ibid., 236.

94. Broderick and Jennings, "Mindfulness for Adolescents," 136.

95. Goodwin, "Obsessed with Governance," 36–46; Shoul and Rabinowitz, "Building Hope in a De-Industrializing Community," 36–47.

ity to deal well with what's really going on."[96] Margaret Wheatley explains that the "real world" is an interconnected network of living systems. The fundamental "building blocks are relationships, not individuals."[97] In addition, hierarchical systems foster fear that, in turn, reduces identification with the group and inhibits cooperation.[98] An atmosphere of attention to one another, "in tune" and mindful of all members of the group, makes self-organized group leadership feasible.

The Parameters of Group Discernment

Discernment is rooted in distinctly Christian principles.[99] It is the act of perceiving "in the absence of judgment with a view to obtaining spiritual direction and understanding."[100] Mindfulness practice in a leadership group is an invitation to reflect and be attentive, listening with imagination—a present-moment disposition of curiosity and openness to the Spirit—together. Group mindfulness acknowledges that practicing mindfulness is not a solitary act. It is done in the context of space and time, in a social setting. It is *incorporative* and *excorporative*, that is, the practice occurs *for/in* the individual in time and body, while also being *for* the group. So while the practice is individual, each member practices in the presence of one another, sharing the same goal, finding common meaning and purpose.[101]

Group Identity Formation and Community

Individuals develop identity within the context of a social system. The structure of a social system influences the strength of an individual's identification with that culture. Interestingly, persons of collectivistic cultures tend to identify more strongly with the culture *and* develop a stronger sense of self than those raised in individualistic cultures.[102] A greater sense

96. Wheatley, "Self-Organized Networks," 7.

97. Ibid.

98. Zagefka and Jamir, "Conflict, Fear and Social Identity in Nagaland," 43–51.

99. Scriptural support for discernment include, Ps 139:2; Prov 1:5; Rom 12:2; 1 Cor 2:14–15; 1 Cor 12:10. See also "In Our Own Language," in chapter 2 above.

100. *New Oxford American Dictionary*.

101. Nilsson, "A Four-Dimensional Model of Mindfulness and Its Implications for Health," 165.

102. Becker et al., "Culture and the Distinctiveness Motive," 848.

of belonging, which is most often found in collectivistic cultures, has the correlative effect of greater well-being and life satisfaction. Members of these cultures feel more valued and secure, released to find space for self-awareness without harsh judgment. These more secure individuals are, in turn, unconstrained and thus contribute more creatively to the community (recall the *perichoresis* in chapter two). In this way, culture of origin affects the perceived coherence (or lack thereof) in a group setting where multiple cultures are represented.[103]

Human beings come to know others, in general, based on personal experiences (personality, current state, etc.) and from one's cultural perspective. When two individuals are similar, this is not a problem. However, when there is any difference between individuals, conflict arising from biases such as prejudice and/or envy is common.[104] Identification with members of a group, group cohesion, and proclivity for empathy between members may prove elusive. But mindfulness practiced in a group context is shown to increase the possibility for empathy.

One way to measure identification with, and empathy toward, another is to study the behavioral and neurological markers that indicate envy, specifically in the competitive atmosphere of a group. In general, when one feels happy from having just experienced a win, others are perceived in a positive light. It is equally common to find that, when one is unhappy (e.g., just experienced a loss), others are perceived as bearing negative attributes. Envy, and its darker companion, *schadenfreude* (the pleasure one derives from the misfortune of another), arises out of social comparison. Envy occurs when one who has lost at something feels worse upon witnessing another's win. *Schadenfreude*, then, occurs when the person who wins feels better upon witnessing the loss of another. Both impact the extent to which group identity formation and community might occur.

The authors of one study were interested in the mechanism that determines whether the same processes occur when an individual projects the emotional state of envy or *schadenfreude* on another who has experienced a win or loss. Researchers Nikolaus Steinbeis and Tania Singer regard the distinction as important because it "highlights the myriad ways in which socio-affective judgments can be subject to biases."[105] These biases are

---

103. Tsukamoto et al., "Cultural Differences in Perceived Coherence of the Self and Ingroup," 83–89.

104. Steinbeis and Singer, "Projecting My Envy onto You," 370.

105. Ibid., 372.

crucial aspects of mindful attention in a social group. Without reflection, egocentric bias will cloud judgment and inhibit collaboration and communication. The area of the brain that processes the feelings of envy (e.g., anterior insula) is activated rather than the region triggered during "cognitive perspective taking" (e.g., cortical midline structures). The study found that the degree to which an individual experienced emotions and attributed emotions when personally engaged was significantly correlated to the degree to which the individual *observing* another in the same activity attributed the same emotions.[106]

What is more, Steinbeis and Singer found that direct emotional involvement was not necessary for an egocentric bias to be involved, "and the degree to which one attributes envy or *schadenfreude* to a 3rd party was still correlated with one's own tendency to experience such social emotions in similar situations."[107] That is, "areas involved in the first-hand experience of [higher order] social emotions are . . . recruited when vicariously attributing these emotions to others."[108] Crucially, the degree to which neuronal activity occurred with the personal experience of envy was equal to the activity that occurred upon attributing envy to another.[109] These are very strong, emotionally charged responses and carry significant implications for group cohesion. In settings that set up a win-loss hierarchy of relationships, those more prone to envy and *schadenfreude* experience negative affect toward others. They also personally experience the same affective negativity that is projected when they witness others in the win-loss arrangement.

At the same time, as mentioned above, other studies using neuroimaging confirm corresponding levels of neuronal activation between a personal experience of pain and imagining another's pain.[110] That is, similar mechanisms activated during personal pain are enacted to produce empathy when another is in pain, and the tranquil effect on the synaptic activity is significant. The development of empathy in a group setting is key, and it is critical for maintaining an identity that honors one's socio-cultural heritage. When groups are increasingly diverse in composition, even subtle

---

106. Ibid., 375.
107. Ibid., 378.
108. Ibid., 377.
109. The only departure in all four components of the study found that the neuronal activity associated with *schadenfreude* did not show the same degree of strength (and regions) when compared to attribution of the emotion to another.
110. Singer et al., "Effects of Oxytocin and Prosocial Behavior on Brain Responses to Direct and Vicariously Experienced Pain," 788.

behaviors can threaten the strength of an individual's identity and impact the range of influence, for example, of those with historically minority status.[111] An awareness of self and others is particularly salient in diverse social settings, since social cues (physical posture, proximity, gestures, etc.) carry distinctive meaning in different cultures.[112] Group mindfulness practice develops this self and other awareness skill, reducing judgment and increasing acceptance.[113]

Effects of Loneliness

Leadership as it is traditionally modeled by Western individualistic societies is an isolated and isolating position. Leadership training often does not include instruction in developing and maintaining social acuity skills. The result is often an increasingly isolated position that in equal measure isolates the leader from followers. Ineffective and frequently destructive results ensue, reducing the chance for the business (or company, institution, etc.) to succeed. But loneliness has even more dire effects. Those who perceive themselves to be lonely carry morbidity rates nearly twice that of obesity and quadruple for air pollution.[114] Dementia significantly increases with perceived loneliness, as well. In several studies, "controlling for age, IQ, gender, years of education, and social class, only loneliness was associated significantly with changes in IQ."[115] Hierarchical, individualistic leadership serves no one well.

Similar phenomena are observed with self-esteem studies that show that focusing on the self for esteem is counterproductive. When, for example, coaching directs the focus on the *result* (e.g., the effect this behavior has on another person, or what will be accomplished when this task is completed), motivation shifts and self-contentment (i.e., well-being) results.[116]

---

111. Emerson and Murphy, "Identity Threat at Work," 508.

112. The "colorblind" propaganda has the effect of suppressing Black and Latino/a identities and marginalizing cultural distinctiveness rather than incorporating the unique cultural character of each group into a richer social experience. Ibid., 512.

113. Merely providing awareness of stereotypes has been shown to actually increase stereotyping, since it categorizes the difference rather than provoking an openness to and understanding of another culture. Duguid and Thomas-Hunt, "Condoning Stereotyping?" 345.

114. Cacioppo et al., "Toward a Neurology of Loneliness," 1465.

115. Ibid., 1466.

116. Ryan and Brown, "Why We Don't Need Self-Esteem," 71–76.

Put another way, self-esteem as a motivator is self-focused, individualistic, and self-dependent, whereas mindfulness practice, and mindfulness in group practice, is centered on noticing what is happening in order to see it for what it is, producing a sense of well-being. This sensitivity—awareness—predisposes the practitioner to notice what is happening in the surrounding environment.

An unsettling, emerging issue compounding the problem pertains to the pervasive use of mobile devices. In fact, behavioral psychologists are developing a tool to measure "nomophobia," or the fear of being without the use of a mobile device.[117] Of particular concern is that mobile devices are being integrated into the daily functioning for increasing numbers of young people. The study showed that sense of abandonment and isolation from the world is alarmingly pronounced in those (more often than not brief) moments sans phone, making the concerns mentioned above all the more urgent. Group mindfulness practice alongside individual mindfulness practices tends to the crucial skill of reality checking that is essential for the development of healthy, socially adept human beings.

Effects of Group Mindfulness

Attention on others, rather than the self, is more effective and productive in a learning environment. It also may explain why strictly secular mindfulness training does not necessarily have *consistent* long-term effects. Those who maintain enduring mindfulness practices are those whose focus of mindful attention is an Other (i.e., spiritual versus strictly physical), and who separate it from the strictly Buddhist set of principles. The system of self-reference "is a network of thoughts, ideas, definitions, and emotions that organize and constitute much of daily existence for most people." This "self-schema" is not merely a philosophical paradigm. It is "a functional neural network located anatomically in cortical midline brain structures."[118] Focus on the self consistently evokes "less effective skill learning and performance relative to external focus instructions."[119] That is, focus on the self in relation to perceived judgment triggers performance anxieties, threats of stereotypes (race, gender, ability, intelligence), and expectations. These distractions inhibit learning and engagement with the community and en-

---

117. Yildirim and Correia, "Exploring the Dimensions of Nomophobia," 130–37.
118. McKay et al., "The Self: Your Own Worst Enemy?" 39.
119. Ibid., 40.

vironment. The practice of group discernment—mindful of others and the Other—mitigates the distractions.

What is more, a majority of effective mindfulness practices are already incorporated in distinctly Christian religious practices. One set of studies found that self-identified Christians primed by Scripture passages were statistically significantly more cooperative in a group. Those who identified as Hindu or atheist did not show any increase in cooperativeness. It is intriguing that priming people with Hindu passages about cooperation, including those who identified as Hindu, impacted none of the participants. The researchers suggested the reason for this is that, "in the Christian tradition, the formalized and synchronized deployment of musical practices (chanting, instrumentation, singing), integrated with explicit scriptural recitation, and rhythmic swaying and prostrations, may all amplify the effectiveness of texts to alter charitable dispositions and behavior."[120] Integrating distinctly Christian principles of cooperation and sharing into practices that myriad mindfulness training courses use predisposes Christians to the behaviors mindfulness research supports. This may also explain the question raised above concerning the role of a *more-than* in influencing hormone and chemical activity while not changing the mechanism that evolutionary theory should explain.

Cooperation and In-Sync Leadership

To restate, group mindfulness training helps participants expand interpersonal skills. With a common goal, members of the group learn to listen more attentively by being present to one another. Like collaborative music-making, mindfulness generates a shared experience of inner time—what Alfred Schütz has termed a "mutual tuning-in relationship."[121] Mindfulness training evokes the two primary characters of empathy and compassion. Practiced in a group setting, these characteristics are amplified, making collaboration more likely and more creative.

---

120. Rand et al., "Religious Motivations for Cooperation," 48. It is only one study, and does *not* mean that other principles such as those found in Buddhism are not useful *in addition* to Christian practices.

121. Nilsson, "A Four-Dimensional Model of Mindfulness and Its Implications for Health," 165. See also Schutz, "Making Music Together," in Brodersen, *Collected Papers II Social Theory*, 159–178.

Working together toward a common goal, humans are also more likely to balance resources with a fair, egalitarian process. Using computer games to emulate situations that require the distribution of resources, researchers can observe a variety of mechanisms that underlie cooperation. One such study kept individuals anonymous to each other to prevent interference from reputation and prejudice. Participants generally worked to allocate more funds to those with fewer resources and penalize those with exceptionally greater resources.[122] Per research design, allocative means were costly, which meant there was little incentive to choose that option.[123] And because there was no payoff for revenge and reimbursement, those factors did not influence individuals' motivations. When teasing out the emotion behind people's reaction to inequality, researchers found that "individuals apparently feel negative emotions towards high earners and the intensity of these emotions increases with income inequality."[124] When status and superficial differences are no longer a factor, people tend to cooperate and respond with negative emotions to inequality.

Another related study measured the contagiousness of selfish and cooperative behaviors in fixed versus fluid dynamic networks. When individuals have little or no control over their networks, selfishness and cooperation are contagious. That is, individuals are more likely to adopt a neighbor's behavior. In fluid networks, selfish behavior was contagious, but cooperation was not. The researchers who conducted this longitudinal study, however, found that, over time, cooperation became more normative. The implication is that when individuals are not confined to static network structures (e.g., hierarchies of incentives) they are more likely to choose to be—*and remain*—cooperative, holding out to attract other cooperative folks.[125] Indeed, cooperative participants grew increasingly less influenced by a selfish neighbor over time, particularly as cooperative participants joined the network. Given freedom to choose network partners, individuals tend to *choose* to develop and maintain cooperative working networks.

A caveat to the holdout among cooperative individuals is that, even if some might be influenced to cooperate in the fixed network system, the immediate payoff is greater for the selfish behavior. More of the suggestible coworkers will choose the selfish coalition, even when, in evolutionary

---

122. Dawes et al., "Egalitarian Motives in Humans," 794.
123. Ibid., 795.
124. Ibid.
125. Jordan et al., "Contagion of Cooperation in Static and Fluid Social Networks," 5.

terms, fitness is highest among cooperators in the long run. Impulsive decision-making may bring immediate gain, but reflection and restraint yield long-term benefit for the individual and the community. Once again, mindfulness practice is significant to a long-term project, such as that of a church, bringing about the highest functioning outcome. Those who engage in mindfulness practices are shown to display greater impulse control and to delay gratification.[126] Mindfulness practices alongside group discernment inherently increase the possibility of people exercising the discipline that a long-range perspective of cooperative action requires. This process is slower than in a system of hierarchical decision-making, but the health and fitness of the organism as a whole is much greater.[127] Otherwise, the system remains static; in other words, it does not grow. Cooperation is key to developing more complexity[128]—the "maturity . . . [of] the measure of the full stature of Christ," as Ephesians 4:13 references.

The Family, Tradition, and Group Leadership

In a related vein, Jon Kabat-Zinn drew heavily on Buddhist concepts when he first developed the MBSR. Buddhist tenets explain that the practice of empathy and compassion begins in the family, then broadens to the community, and finally extends outward into the world. To produce consistent compassion and empathy, the practice must be a daily habit. If it is first directed within the family unit, including the children, the children will in turn develop a habit of the mindfulness practice of compassion, in particular.[129]

Defining compassion is a challenge, particularly if the aim is to intentionally cultivate compassion. To start, consider what compassion *isn't*. *Apathy* stems from the objectification of the other in a relationship. When the other is seen as an object, emotional connection is nonexistent. The other is less important, and an imbalance of power occurs, which is

---

126. Areni and Black, "Consumers' Responses to Small Portions," 532–43; McCarthy and Wald, "Mindfulness and Good Enough Sex," 39–47.

127. In complex, multilevel systems, the distinctions are nuanced, though, given the choice, cooperation usually wins out in the majority of cases. See Nowak, "Five Rules for the Evolution of Cooperation," 5805.

128. Fu and Nowak, "Global Migration Can Lead to Stronger Spatial Selection Than Local Migration," 638.

129. Nilsson, "A Four-Dimensional Model of Mindfulness and Its Implications for Health," 166.

objectification in the extreme case. *Antipathy* does involve emotion, but it is negative, and sometimes includes strong emotion. *Sympathy* feels the suffering of another but lacks the true emotional connection to the one who suffers (i.e., is condescending). Contra the Buddhist sense of *empathy*, the general Western practice of empathy involves an understanding of another's pain to the extent that one identifies pathologically with it—that is, one identifies to the degree that holy indifference is not possible and can actually hinder healing and health. An "authentic human encounter" is a kind of empathy that is true compassion,[130] and *it is* found in the practice of holy indifference described above.

Compassionate love is related to the concept of compassion but goes further by encompassing the desire to give of oneself in the effort to alleviate the suffering of another, as well as to help the other thrive.[131] In the case of parenting when the situation is especially stressful, compassion is difficult to come by. Mercifully, "mindfulness training aimed at cultivating compassion has been shown to decrease parental stress . . . and improve the quality of parenting and parent-child relationships."[132] Stress triggers avoidance behavior and is injurious to a compassionate relationship. Compassionate love, however, is shown to increase warmth and positive parenting during a stressful situation and even protect against the overactive sympathetic nervous system (SNS). But, in the Miller et al., study, compassion training alone did not consistently predict physiologic regulation of the autonomic nervous system (ANS). Intentional mindfulness training, however, does cultivate compassion and bolsters that consistency.[133]

The growing field of contemplative science is interested in the feature of compassion as it relates to mindfulness practice. The emerging view defines "mindfulness and compassion . . . as intrinsic, though limited, capacities of human beings that can be 'extended' through intentional training and education toward certain end-states."[134] The premise is that mindfulness practice in some form is crucial to the formation of human

---

130. Ibid., 167–168.

131. Miller et al., "Compassionate Love Buffers Stress-Reactive Mothers from Fight-or-Flight Parenting," 36. This definition for compassionate love is virtually identical with the operational term *altruism* for the researcher in the section, "Mindfulness Research," above.

132. Ibid., 36. See also Benn et al., "Mindfulness Training Effects for Parents and Educators of Children with Special Needs," 48.

133. Ibid., 41.

134. Roeser and Eccles, "Mindfulness and Compassion in Human Development," 2.

relationships, development, and education. Scientists and educators are increasingly of the opinion that, in the very least, the system of education should incorporate instruction in and the practice of mindfulness. Indeed, research from a Taiwanese social learning project supports the assertion that mindful reflection coupled with compassionate action is significantly meaningful for college students.[135] Reaching these teachable young people with wonderfully moldable neuropathways, and training Christian leadership in such practices, is a good strategy.

Many of the mindfulness practices used with clinically high efficacy are, in some form, already integrated in family rituals (predominantly associated with organized religion). Increasingly, young people are noticing the lack of such rituals and expressing a desire to reenact them. At the same time, in another study involving college students, "a 'caring' parenting style was the only significant predictor of the meaningfulness of rituals."[136] As noted above, compassion is key to meaningful relationships, and is the stimulus to perpetuate the development of meaningful relationships with others. And, since mindfulness practice is shown to nurture compassion, intentionally employing mindful attention in the context of family religious ritual is intuitive.[137]

Identity is first shaped in the context of the family, in whatever form that might take, and parenting style—the parent-child relationship, in particular—holds a great deal of influence over that development. Specifically, "when individuals grow up with autonomy-thwarting parents, they may be prevented from exploring internally endorsed values and identities and as a result shut out aspects of the self perceived to be unacceptable."[138] Parental

---

135. Su et. al., "Encountering Selves and Others," 43.

136. Friedman and Weissbrod, "Attitudes Toward the Continuation of Family Rituals Among Emerging Adults," from the abstract. See also Marks, "Sacred Practices in Highly Religious Families," 217–31.

137. Corporal punishment and authoritative parenting in any context is shown to engender negative affect toward family tradition and rituals. See Khoury-Kassabri, "Attitudes of Arab and Jewish Mothers Towards Punitive and Non-Punitive Discipline Methods," 135–44; Ellison and Bradshaw, "Religious Beliefs, Sociopolitical Ideology, and Attitudes Toward Corporal Punishment," 320–40; Ben-Arieh and Haj-Yahia, "Corporal Punishment of Children," 687–95; Coatsworth et al., "Integrating Mindfulness with Parent Training," 26–35. For the use of spiritual mindfulness practices in the context of secular institutions such as schools, camps, and the YMCA, see Benson et al., "Spiritual Development."

138. Weinstein et al., "Parental Autonomy Support and Discrepancies Between Implicit and Explicit Sexual Identities," from the abstract.

support of healthy autonomy is key to the development of "personal integrity, well-being, and positive functioning."[139] And mindfulness practices play a significant role in providing the conditions for the parent to be self-aware and child-aware, and to then bolster the healthy development of the same in their children.

Identifying the existence of the family—with its unique opportunities and challenges—is important to the infrastructure of the community of a church. Leadership in the setting of the church is leadership to the family. Every culture is concerned about the health and development of children, and the family is the most obvious place to concentrate greater effort. When the leadership of a church practices leadership in a discerning, mindful way, other members of the church will know the effects.

It is also true that leadership calls for courage alongside compassion. Issues for within the family and for individuals are personal and, when exposed, leave members vulnerable. To lead, one must have a strong sense of self-awareness and well-being, while also being open to the character of another—in other words, cooperative. These are characteristics that have traditionally been segregated by sex-type categorizations, with many expressing preference for the stereotypic masculine traits. Both are clearly needed for the healthiest and highest functioning outcomes to occur in increasingly complex situations. Truly, courage, compassion, and cooperative behavior need not be classified other than by virtue of being necessary for a thriving human community.

CONCLUSION

While it is not necessary to grasp the complexities of neural pathways to change habits, increase focus, or work collaboratively and effectively in leadership, better understanding of the processes offers improved tools for individuals and groups to engage in order to mature. Advances in these sciences help the practitioner train others to more effectively make healthier connections in the brain that effect behavior and spirituality. It is ironic that many leaders in Western corporate business have implemented other-honoring collaborative-style management ahead of the institutional church.[140] Companies such as Facebook and Apple embrace an open workspace and

---

139. Ibid., 815.

140. See for instance, DePree, *Leadership Is an Art*; Collins, *Good to Great and the Social Sectors*; Morse, *Making Room for Leadership*.

collaborative decision-making. Twitter and Zappos, among others, now use a system of *Holacracy* that encourages "dynamic roles" and "distributed authority" to run their companies.[141] Still, the practices are already in the DNA of the ancient church, and perhaps all that the information-flooded brains of contemporary Christians need is knowledge of the science behind what the spirit has known from the beginning.

---

141. Robertson and Thomison, "Holacracy."

4

Research Question and Design

This chapter is included here for a couple of reasons. First, many readers will appreciate the quantitative research process and findings because you genuinely welcome numbers and would like to see how I measured the effectiveness of mindfulness spiritual practice as a leadership style. The qualitative method I used is *especially important* to the purpose of this book because it begins to analyze the phenomenon, the nature of the system that underlies how we perceive good leadership. Things change only when we understand why things are as they are. Otherwise, we are doomed to plaster new programs over older programs, while the institution remains static inevitably followed by entropy.

HYPOTHESIS

As mindfulness attention and greater acceptance (openness) to members in a leadership group increase, members will identify to a greater degree with androgynous personality characteristics after a fourteen-week mindfulness attention skills training and group discernment practice program.

Research Question and Design

RESEARCH QUESTION

Will implementing a seven-session program for mindfulness skills training and group discernment practice yield greater identification with more androgynous personality characteristics for individuals in Christian leadership?

THE MINDFULNESS ATTENTION SKILLS TRAINING AND GROUP DISCERNMENT PRACTICE PROGRAM

Timeline

The Mindfulness Attention Skills Training and Group Discernment Practice (MAST-GDP) program was accomplished in seven one-hour sessions over the course of fourteen weeks.

Project Description and Implementation

The MAST-GDP program took place at the First United Methodist Church of Downers Grove, Illinois. The participants included the Administrative Board members and associates, including three individuals from nearby ministries and from a Free Methodist denomination church plant. The sessions were live-streamed using Livestream Producer software and a laptop computer to two additional groups of participants. One group was comprised of leaders of an Episcopal church in Aurora, Illinois; the second was a group of student leaders of a Loyola University ministry program. All groups were convenience samples by virtue of having a connection to the researcher.

Examples of individual mindfulness practices were demonstrated during each of the seven sessions and instructions given to set aside a discrete time for daily practice. A blank calendar was provided for recording the days practiced and the time committed to the practice. Each group practice built on the last, culminating in the practice of a group discernment model developed by John Anderson, "Listening to God Together." See appendix A for a sample.

During the initial session, an excerpt was read from chapter one of *Urban Mindfulness*, "Meditation at Home."[1] Each session began with an in-

---

1. Kaplan, *Urban Mindfulness*, 10–13.

vitation to stillness and quiet with the aid of a chime. The invitation started with attention to breath and posture. Next, participants were instructed to "listen for the space when the sound ends and the silence begins—that is where we are most able to hear the voice of the Spirit," followed by the chime. Samples of the session lesson plans can be found in appendix A. Group practices, by session, went as follows:

Session 1

The focus was to instruct in centering prayer (see appendix A, "The Method of Centering Prayer"). To prepare for this, a body scan practice was introduced to help individuals systematically pay attention to different parts of their bodies. It is a way to reduce habitual mind-wandering and strengthen their momentary awareness of body sensations (appendix A, "Body Scan/ Progressive Body Awareness" script). A Biblical bases for these practices can be seen in Jesus' admonition against striving for temporal matters and the invitation to seek those of the kingdom in Matthew 6:32–34 underpin his subsequent admonition against passing judgment against others (Matt 7:1–5). His point is that, in order to actively share in the greater good (i.e., the kingdom of God), one must first recognize what is going on inside. Attention to and awareness of the body, alongside centering prayer, increases the possibility that the Spirit of God reveals what first needs to be done within.

Session 2

Parker Palmer's "Circle of Trust" (appendix A, "Circle of Trust") was delineated to make clear the "touchstones"—characteristics—of a trusting group. This was followed by an imaginative prayer exercise, a guided prayer using a passage of Scripture to encourage creative listening. It is a precursor to the *lectio divina* practice.[2] Wonder is made possible by arousing the imagination. Scripture declares that God's works are *wonders* (e.g., Deut 6:22; 7:19; 26:8; 29:3, 24), and God's love is *wonder*ful, surpassing sexual love (2 Sam 1:26). Unconditional love is the basis for healthy community. At the same time, healthy community confesses to one another (James 5:16), is committed to meeting regularly (Heb 10:22–25), and is only viable if the group

---

2. Oestreicher and Warner, *Imaginative Prayer for Youth Ministry*, 52–53. The "Mother Eagle," a prayer referencing Exod 19:4; Deut 32:10, 11; and Ps 57:1.

Session 3

The focus was on the Mennonite "Holy Spaces of Inclusion" paradigm (Is 61:1–2; Eph 3:18–19),[3] followed by a practice session on the two-minute prayer-reflection (appendix A, "Two-Minute Drill: Group Discernment"). Once inner listening is developing and the parabolic log removed from the eye, there is more freedom to hear and notice the movement of God in others. The two-minute drill practice of discernment develops in people the skill of hearing with others and for one another.

Session 4

The initial instruction briefly covered the mindful strategies for facing cravings (e.g., RAIN: Recognize, Accept, Investigate, and Note mind-states, emotions, and body sensations from moment to moment).[4] Next, the emphasis was to instruct and guide in *lectio divina* (appendix A, "*Lectio Divina* Bookmark"). The mindfulness practices that facilitate attention and awareness without judgment in each moment are paralleled in *lectio divina*. In the spiritual reading of Scripture, the participant pays attention to the words, becomes aware of a word or phrase the Spirit impresses, notices how that phrase can be lived out, and is released to live out of that communion.

Session 5

Teaching was concentrated on attention to and awareness of the environment—that which is situated outside the self (appendix A, "Mindfulness of the External World"). Instruction in Thomas Keating's *visio divina* followed (appendix A, "*Visio Divina* and Iconography"). Jesus encourages faith by reminding his followers to see the beauty of the lilies clothed in splendor and to notice the birds' provisions. Attention to the environment

---

3. Harader, "Holy Spaces of Inclusion," 68. Also, on the idea of "making space" for the self and one another, Lefebvre, *The Production of Space*, 2–4.

4. Brewer et. al., "Craving to Quit," 77–78.

and praying with the visual aid of a prayer icon invites the participant to notice the beauty of God's movement, and to have eyes to see God in others.

Session 6

The final instructions directed the attention of the small group participants to a salient issue for the group. The bulk of the hour was devoted to guiding the participants through the group discernment protocol (appendix A, "Listening to God Together"). Making decisions as a group, discerning the movement of the Spirit together, is the crux of the narrative of chapter four of Ephesians. Spiritual practices that facilitate personal mindfulness and awareness of each other make the practice of group discernment achievable.

Testing and Observation Procedure

Quantitative Method

Participants were asked to join the study either directly by the researcher or by a secondary referral by others known to the researcher, including a plea on Facebook. Each group was given disclosures and permission forms to sign that included the option to discontinue if so desired. The MAAS, BSRI, GHS, preliminary questions regarding current mindfulness attention practices, and demographics questionnaires were administered via Survey Monkey (with hard copies available to those without computer access) before the start of the intervention.[5] The corresponding number to data set were encrypted, and data linked to a random participant. Each group participated in seven one-hour training sessions. The first session was introductory and outlined the agenda of the following six sessions. During each session, the participants received instruction in various independent mindful practices using handouts and/or mobile apps.[6] A calendar was also provided for participants to use to keep track of the number and duration of personal meditation sessions. Additionally, each participant received an every-other day cell phone text that included a picture and prayer phrase as

---

5. Several studies show no variation "in the performance or psychometric properties of various psychological measures administered via paper-and-pencil and computer-based modalities." Jislin-Goldberg et. al., "Mindfulness and Positive Affect," 7.

6. See Contemplative Outreach, "Centering Prayer Mobile App." See also appendix B, "Resources—Mobile Apps."

a prompt for centering prayer. At the conclusion of the seven sessions, the initial survey was re-administered with the same procedure. The Livestream Producer program also recorded each session for an unbiased review of the actual presentation.

Qualitative Method

A compound phenomenon insists on a multifaceted research methodology. For this reason, I used a mixed-methods approach to better understand those complexities of processes and systems.[7] The project and research outlined in this thesis are based on the supposition that knowing the impact of stereotyped expectations on leadership will *lead to action that institutes change*. Issues of power and social relationship also substantiate the importance of the study. As such, the research is based on a *transformative* interpretive framework. A phenomenological theoretical approach was used, as the research aimed to tease out the essence of the phenomena that influence expectations for leaders and the appropriateness of ascribed characteristics to what is considered good leadership. Additionally, the research sought to bring "to the fore the experiences and perceptions of individuals from their own perspectives, and therefore challenge structural or normative assumptions."[8]

As researcher, I was not committed to one system of philosophy.[9] The perspective was postmodern in its effort to seek answers from multiple perspectives (versus restricting individuals to categories), and the phenomenological approach is effective "at challenging structural or normative assumptions. [So] adding an interpretive dimension to phenomenological research, enabling it to be used as the basis for practical theory, allows it to inform, support or challenge policy and action."[10] A focus group interview with a small group of participants was conducted. The group of five individuals was interviewed before and three remaining at the conclusion of the program (two from DGFUMC, and one from the Free Methodist church plant) about their experiences and responses to components of the program and relevant issues and procedural questions. The researcher took

---

7. Fetters et. al., "Achieving Integration in Mixed Methods Designs-Principles and Practices," pt. 2.
   8. Nesbitt, DMR-801 Research & Methodology Seminar, Denver Seminary.
   9. Creswell, *Qualitative Inquiry & Research Design*, 23.
   10. Stan Lester, "An Introduction to Phenomenological Research," ¶1.

note of changes in perspective on leadership as a result of individual and group mindfulness practice. The following questions shaped the interviews:

The central question: What does it mean to be an effective (aka, "good") leader? The subquestions used to clarify and elicit structural influences were:

1. Issues subquestions: (a) What does a good leader do? What does good leadership look like? (b) What do good leaders not do? What does bad leadership look like? (c) What does a person who exemplifies the term *effective leader* do? (d) What is difficult or easy about being a good leader?

2. Procedural subquestions: (a) What are the structural (sociological/anthropological) meanings of effective leadership? (b) What are the underlying themes and contexts that account for this view of effective leadership (e.g., stereotypic masculine-type characteristics)? (c) What values in Western culture are behind what is expected of "good" leaders?

3. Additional artifacts: (a) smartphone pictures/texts as centering prayer suggestions and reminders (not the smartphone pictures of representations/symbols of a good or bad leader and good or bad leadership planned in the Proposal for the Professional Project), and (b) a calendar log of personal mindfulness practice sessions.

Instrumentation

To measure the strength of the impact the MAST-GDP program has on the group participants, the Mindful Attention Awareness Scale (MAAS) was administered pretest and posttest.

> The trait MAAS is a 15-item scale designed to assess a core characteristic of mindfulness: . . . a receptive state of mind in which attention, informed by a sensitive awareness of what is occurring in the present, simply observes what is taking place. This is in contrast to the conceptually driven mode of processing, in which events and experiences are filtered through cognitive appraisals, evaluations, memories, beliefs, and other forms of cognitive manipulation. . .
> . Internal consistency levels (Cronbach's alphas) generally range from .80 to .90. The MAAS has demonstrated high test-retest reliability, discriminant and convergent validity, known-groups

validity, and criterion validity. Correlational, quasi-experimental, and experimental studies have shown that the trait MAAS taps a unique quality of consciousness that is related to, and predictive of, a variety of emotion regulation, behavior regulation, interpersonal, and well-being phenomena.[11]

A number of factors support the use of the MAAS and substantiate the assumption that a difference in personality expression is reasonable to expect. Personality traits can be changed by volition. Trait personality is modified in part by changes in behaviors related to the general personality in view.[12] Personality traits also change with age.[13] And, while values are shaped in part by culture and generally considered stable, personal values are subject to change as well.[14] Awareness is a key factor, alongside a clear connection with the object of the new value in question. Challenges to values are usually met with resistance, but mindfulness practice that elicits an awareness of automatic reactions and thoughts about that value brings an openness to reconsidering the value (e.g., holding it loosely, without judgment). There is some variation in strength of identification that is dependent on whether the originating culture is individualistic or collectivistic. Even so, the construct validity of the MAAS is consistently reliable in three cultures.[15]

Sandra L. Bem created the Bem Sex Role Inventory (BSRI) to measure the degree to which an individual identifies with the culturally ascribed attributes of a given gender role. The BSRI is composed of 60 personality characteristics: 20 masculine (such as competitive, forceful), 20 feminine (such as understanding, warm), and 20 neutral (such as happy, sincere). Participant were asked to indicate on a seven-point Likert scale (from "never or almost never true" or to "always or almost always true") the extent to which each characteristic describes them. Since the inventory was first developed in 1975, women increasingly identify more with masculine role characteristics, and men indicate identification with more feminine-type role characteristics, though to a lesser degree. The result reveals that the

11. From the permissions statement by the coauthor of the MAAS, and further validity references found in Brown and Ryan, "The Benefits of Being Present," 24; Carlson Brown, "Validation of the Mindful Attention Awareness Scale in a Cancer Population," 29–33.
12. Hudson and Fraley, "Volitional Personality Trait Change," 490–507.
13. Roberts and Mroczek, "Personality Trait Change in Adulthood," 31–35.
14. Bardi and Goodwin, "The Dual Route to Value Change," 273.
15. See the public permissions letter Mindful Attention Awareness Scale (MAAS).

dichotomy of male-female sex role characteristics is narrowing.[16] Still, for the purposes of this study, the difference is sufficient to indicate the possibility for a measure of change in sex-role identification at the end of the six-week program compared with pretest scores.[17]

Bem developed the BSRI according to gender schema theory, which states that individuals organize identity and behaviors around what is perceived as culturally appropriate for one's sex-type.[18] While social learning theory and cognitive development theory both aim to explain personality type development, the premise for gender identity is that "a person's sexual self concept has a significant effect on how that person processes and interprets information."[19] The BSRI has consistently been shown to reliably expose the strength in direction of sex-type self-concept. Additionally, other inventories developed since measure construct validity against the BSRI, and confirms its convergent validity. For instance, the Conformity to Masculine Norms Inventory-46 (CMNI-46) measures the specific identification with stereotypic masculine characteristics, which is relevant to the ultimate thrust of this thesis.[20] The CMNI-46 is shown to possess construct validity against the BSRI but also reliably determines relative levels of self-esteem, which is not relevant to this study. Therefore, the BSRI remained the best choice for measuring sex-type self-concept for this research project.

The Group Cohesiveness Scale (GCS) is a seven-item questionnaire using a five-point Likert-type scale ("strongly agree" to "strongly disagree"). The GCS is shown to be reliable and consistently valid, and is used regularly to assess the effectiveness of psychiatric group programs.[21] The GCS was

16. Berger and Krahé, "Negative Attributes Are Gendered Too," 517; Verhofstadt and Weytens, "Biological Sex and Gender Role Identity as Predictors of Spousal Support Provision," 166–77.

17. Oswald, "An Examination of the Current Usefulness of the Bem Sex-Role Inventory," part 2.

18. Bem, "Gender Schema Theory," 88.

19. Schertzer et al., "A Cross-Cultural Validation of a Gender Role Identity Scale in Marketing," 313.

20. Parent et al., "Evidence of Construct Distinctiveness for Conformity to Masculine Norms," 354. Other tools include the Gender Role Conflict Scale (GRCS), the Positive-Negative Sex Role Inventory (PN-SRI), and Berger and Krahé, "Negative Attributes Are Gendered Too," 516–531.

21. Wongpakaran et al., "The Group Cohesiveness Scale (GCS) for Psychiatric Inpatients," 516–531. Also see Marmarosh et al., "Group Cohesiveness, Group-Derived Collective Self-Esteem, Group-Derived Hope, and the Well-Being of Group Therapy Members," 32–44.

included to measure the degree to which individuals cooperate in making leadership decisions. While group cohesion was not the primary factor to be measured, high group identification is shown to promote a strong sense of personal control and identity[22] and would, in turn, reinforce the importance of group mindfulness synchronization as it relates to shifts in gender identification.

Validity Concerns

The power of priming is significant for many reasons. Priming, activating an association in memory prior to a task, is a valuable technique for testing the strength of influence a concept has in a given situation.[23] But it can also unintentionally detract or skew results, sacrificing external validity. What is more, state mindfulness is difficult to assess if the measures are administered remotely (e.g., the State Mindfulness Scale).[24] At the same time, trait mindfulness is more affective and emotion-based, and thus more difficult to assess with precision. The MAAS shows strong validity and reliability over time, measured against other tools and accounting for bias. Still, the influence of priming is real and may have skewed initial scores. The difference between pretest and posttest scores was expected to be sufficient to confirm the reliability of the MAAS to measure change in mindful awareness and attention.

Self-report measures, in general, are prone to bias, particularly for those with a strong desire to augment self-impression. There is between-culture variance in the compulsion to self-enhance (versus a commitment to realism). The difficulty is discerning whether self-promotion reflects a high level of well-being or compensation for the opposite.[25] Whether the use of the Life Satisfaction Index (LSI) to increase the validity of the self-report scores was prudent for this study was considered. The LSI is shown to have satisfactory concurrent validity with other measures of life satisfaction and acceptable internal consistency ($\alpha = .76$).[26] In the end, it

22. Greenaway et al., "From 'We' to 'Me,'" 1–18.2015, (2015

23. Bardi and Goodwin, "The Dual Route to Value Change: Individual Processes and Cultural Moderators," 271–87.

24. Jislin-Goldberg et. al., "Mindfulness and Positive Affect," 349–61.

25. Kim et al., "Cultural Differences in Self- and Other-Evaluations and Well-Being," 857.

26. Rintala, "Predictive Validity of Social Support Relative to Psychological

was apparent the survey was already quite expansive and the number of participants small enough to evaluate confounding influences that might affect test results.

Data Analysis Procedures

It was not feasible to employ a random sampling, so three groups from different locations (i.e., demographics) was used to expand the range of the population sampled and provide the possibility for comparison between groups.[27] According to Cohen's power table, the number needed for a quantitative test with a power of .8, a probability of .05, and a middle effect size is 45–60 participants.[28] Around fifty participants were expected, but only twenty-three individuals competed the entire program. With two Independent Variables (mindfulness and group discernment) and one Dependent Variable (sex stereotype), a two-way dependent ANOVA would serve to determine the significance of the intervention.[29] Before running the complex two-way dependent ANOVA a paired samples t-test was performed on the Bem Sex Role Inventory pretest and posttest scores.

For the interviews, data was collected using the iPad app Interview Assistant (version 1.0.2). For the data analysis of the interviews, the Computer Assisted Qualitative Data Analysis Software (CAQDAS) Atlas.ti[30] was used to code and process the interview data pretest and posttest.

Anticipated Results and Benefits

At the end of a seven-session, fourteen-week program for mindfulness skills training and group discernment practice, it was expected that the individuals in the Christian leadership group would show an increase in mindful awareness and attention from pretest to posttest on the MAAS. It was also expected that individuals would indicate a stronger identification with androgynous personality characteristics on the BSRI in posttest scores when compared to pretests scores. Last, while not the primary aim of

---

Well-Being in Men with Spinal Cord Injury," 424.
- 27. Davies, *Doing a Successful Research Project*, 55.
- 28. Cohen, "A Power Primer," 112.
- 29. Davies, 247.
- 30. See Atlasti Qualitative Data Analysis Software.

this research project, it was expected that the group members would show evidence of the development of characteristics that suggest greater group cohesion (e.g., a willingness to cooperate, collaborate, and listen, more creative ideas, etc.).

Leadership paradigms continue to expect leaders to exhibit stereotypic masculine characteristics, and yet, according to role congruency theory, men and women tend to be more at ease in gender congruous roles.[31] In more general terms, it was anticipated that mindful practice as part of a group discernment leadership paradigm would produce two primary benefits: (1) stress would be alleviated by mere participation in mindful awareness practices, and (2) group mindful practice and shared discernment would alleviate a perceived need for a strictly masculine-type leadership style, which would result in cooperative direction. The second benefit would also ease stress. Since stress triggers hormones and chemicals that provoke competitive, rigid behaviors, the risk for such behaviors is reduced.

In the church leadership setting, the potential benefits are seemingly limitless. Church members and those who observe the church (e.g., those in the same neighborhood of the church building, or family and friends of church members) follow the lead of those who are in leadership positions. The leadership board that cooperates and makes unified decisions is exceedingly more attractive than one that bickers and undermines co-members, and this makes its leadership more effective. The research suggests that mindful awareness and cooperative leadership will result in collaboration with members of the community at large. Moreover, many studies show the correlative effects of "intergenerational attraction" and mindfulness practice, which further emphasizes the benefit of strengthening relationships across generations and within families.[32] And the benefits that research suggests issue from mindful awareness practice will extend to the church community.

A church community that collaborates and grows in unity—to the "measure of the full stature of Christ"—will be more concerned for the well-being of the surrounding community. It is possible that attendance would increase, but this was not the aim of the project. Rather, the anticipated outcome was healthy leadership that practices the presence of God in the presence of one another, and a leadership paradigm that release individual members to be who each one is most truly as created in God's image.

31. Koenig et al., "Are Leader Stereotypes Masculine?" 637.
32. See for example, Haas and Langer, "Mindful Attraction and Synchronization," 31.

The operation of each as congruent selves, as in Parker Palmer's "undivided life," should release the leadership group to operate to its fullest capacity. Such a group, if such results ensue, has the potential to be the model for other church leadership groups. The most salient outcome anticipated was to affect some measure of influence on the more traditional leadership style employed by a majority of Western churches. It is uncontested that overall church membership has long been on the decline. Those in leadership bear the bulk of the responsibility.

5

Results

QUANTITATIVE DATA

THE PROJECT DETAILED IN chapter 4 was developed to explore the impact of mindfulness practice and group leadership training on identification with stereotypic sex role attributes in leadership groups. Observation of, and experience in leadership, coupled with the research data suggests: (1) stereotypic masculine characteristics continue to pervade expectations church members and leaders maintain that leaders put into action, and (2) attention and thoughtful reflection are increasingly challenged by a surge in development and prevalence of technological devices, and the lifestyle this technology gives license to.

As already established, the Cohen's power table indicates the number needed for a quantitative test with a power of .8, probability of .05, and middle effect size is 45–60 participants. With two Independent Variables (mindfulness and group discernment) and one Dependent Variable (sex stereotype), a two-way dependent ANOVA was designated to determine the significance of the intervention. Due to a number of unforeseen circumstances, of the approximately fifty people who originally indicated a willingness to participate in the research study, only twenty-three completed the course. And of those remaining, twenty actually participated in some or all of the sessions.

The raw data generated by SurveyMonkey suggested that determining the data selection and two-way dependent ANOVA subtests might be irrelevant if there was no statistical significant change in the Dependent Variable, sex stereotype. To determine if such a change occurred, a paired samples t-test was performed on the Bem Sex Role Inventory pretest and posttest scores.[1] There was no significant change between the two BSRI score sets. Therefore, evidence does not exist to reject the null hypothesis.

Since the null hypothesis cannot be rejected, there is a strong possibility the intervention does not effect the level of one's identification with stereotypic sex roles. The results from the pretest and posttest *focus group* interviews, however, *do indicate* a possibility that such change may occur. The results of the focus group interviews and a discussion of the results are included below.

Though the hypothesis of the research thesis was not dependent on the specific scores of the Independent Variables mindfulness and group discernment, discussion of the results of the Mindfulness Attention and Awareness Scale and Group Cohesiveness Scale is still relevant. Of the twenty-three participants, the BSRI scores of eleven indicated a stronger identification with androgynous stereotypic sex roles at the conclusion of the program. There were seven whose scores indicated greater identification with feminine characteristics; of these three were male and four, female. Of the four who scored higher for masculine traits, two were female. Twelve of the twenty-three scored higher on the MAAS. In the case of the GCS data, five respondents' posttest scores indicated greater group cohesion, while four remained the same as pretest scores.

Discussion of the Quantitative Data

Since the research failed to reject the null hypothesis, a Type II error (failure to detect an effect that does exist) may have occurred. The sample size was too small to measure a complex experiment that includes two Independent Variables and one Dependent Variable. The two-way dependent ANOVA was further undermined by a research design that did not include a control

---

1. For more detailed data, charts, and graphs see Snyder, "The Impact of Mindfulness Practice and Group Leadership Training on Identification with Stereotypic Sex Role Attributes in Christian Leadership Groups," 150–61.

Results

group. While the distribution of participants could theoretically provide the data to consign three of the participants to a control group, the sample size is much too small to extract statistical meaning. There are a variety of possible confounding factors that may have influenced the pretest and posttest results of each of the three measures used for this research project. These factors are considered below.

Group Cohesiveness Scale

In the case of the Group Cohesiveness Scale data, five respondents' posttest scores indicated greater group cohesion, while four remained the same as pretest scores. The results for the remaining fourteen showed a decrease in group interconnection. Several conditions might play a part in these less than encouraging results. The most significant reason for the elusiveness of group connection is that there were different group configurations each session. Only five participants attended six to seven sessions at the facility where the program took place. Participation of the remaining fourteen ranged from attending one session with some or all of the rest viewed via LiveStream, to attending five and viewing one or two sessions on-line. Consequently, the small groupings during the sessions comprised a different set of people each time. It is also apparent that the specific questions asked in the GCS were not best suited to measure the degree of group cohesion in the case of this study.

Another factor may involve the nature of perceptions that often develop over time by churchgoers that establish rigid presumptions of one another. When there is familiarity but authentic intimacy is lacking, prejudices often develop in larger groups over time. For example, one participant whose schedule already included daily prayerful mindfulness practices, though known to the researcher was not connected with the church where the program took place. While the newcomer did not change notably in MAAS scores, her sense of being a part of a group (GCS score) notably increased by .571; versus the .142 difference in the other three marks of increase (standard deviation = .464). Since she was not part of a leadership group to start, this increase might indicate that her sense of meaningful belonging was more substantial for her. Whereas the majority of participants that attended the sessions at the church were already familiar with one another, relational expectations might already have been established.

Many of the program practices highlighted the importance of vulnerability and being present to each other (seeing into the others as they truly are); that these were not previously true conditions might have been amplified by the course and their responses more accurately reflected the sense of group cohesion. More participants scored similarly in the posttest. Several attendees *verbally* indicated a greater sense of trust by the end of the course. While there was no statistically significant difference between pretest and posttest GCS scores, the posttest mean scores clustered more closely, possibly indicating an overarching understanding of what group cohesiveness requires.

Further, the circumstances were not ideal for a researcher at the time the project was conducted. By the end of the doctoral program, I was no longer pastoring in the same church as at the beginning. Midway into the coursework, an intentional missional community (i.e., a church plant) was spearheaded, simultaneously ministering in the church in which my husband is youth pastor, where the project took place. Since relationships were new and there was no formal leadership position established at the time, buy-in and any sense of obligation to participate were hard to come by. Assuring one-hour session limits appeared to be the only way to secure commitments to engage the project to its completion. This was not enough time to teach *and practice* mindful awareness and attention within the groups in a significant way. Specifically, the Quaker-inspired "Two-Minute Drill" should be practiced in each session after the initial instruction in the second session. This was a very meaningful exercise at the time and would certainly increase the possibility for group cohesion particularly considering the variable group configurations.

Mindfulness Attention and Awareness Scale

The Mindfulness Attention and Awareness Scale is a well-established measure of mindfulness attention and awareness. At the same time, the parametric data is based on controlled research settings. Such controls were not as available to the researcher at the time of the research project, making room for confounding variables. The most significant of these confounds is a risk that all self-report type measures share: conflated self-report bias.[2] After taking the pretest, several people privately admitted that they might

---

2. See for example, Donaldson and Grant-Vallone, "Understanding Self-Report Bias in Organizational Behavior Research," 245–60.

Results

have overestimated their actual level of mindfulness. As in the case of group cohesiveness, after taking the course, members learned more precisely what mindfulness practices are and experienced the effects of intentional attention and awareness. Education and greater proficiency may have increased the possibility for a more accurate sense of their state of mindful awareness and attention. Consequently, these same participants may have indicated a more accurate score for their level of mindfulness in the MAAS posttest.

One participant, however, was a model member and an exception to the confounding factors. This woman was in a profession that is often stressful, requiring her to make quick decisions and work extra hours when needed. To track her high blood pressure she wore a Fitbit activity and heart rate tracker. During one particularly stressful meeting she noticed the signs of stress, noted her heart rate, and began a centering prayer and breathing exercise. After fifteen minutes her heart rate decreased by twenty beats per minute. Several weeks later she was in a serious car accident. By employing the body-scan mindfulness exercise she learned in the first session, she was able to manage her pain more effectively and could more accurately describe to her attending physicians where she hurt, leading to more effective treatment. The MAAS posttest score of this model member signified the greatest increase of all the participants (1.88). This person's case is the only one of two known to the researcher in which the mindfulness awareness and attention prayer practices were regularly applied. In the second case, the participant set a daily alarm on her phone to remind her to practice centering prayer. The MAAS posttest score of this second woman was also greater, though to a lesser degree (0.28).

At the same time, the MAAS t-score did indicate a statistical significant change. Since mindfulness was an independent variable and not the dependent variable hypothesized in this research, it cannot be formally considered as a successful result of the study. The positive change does support, however, one component of the research project: consistently engaging in mindfulness practices is likely to increase mindful attention and awareness.

While the MAAS Posttest scores did not retain the highest average scores, the overall scores clustered in greater frequency at a higher level. This may indicate an overarching understanding of what mindfulness attention and awareness requires and provides.

Bem Sex Role Inventory

Another compounding issue that may affect the results of the surveys used in this study is that by administering the pretest and posttest online via the SurveyMonkey Internet platform, there was no control over when the tests would be taken. When the test is administered at the end of the last session, but while members are still present and the experience fresh on their minds, participants are more likely to respond with answers positively correlated to the course objectives. When given the choice, most people will fit the test in when convenient, even if it is at a time when conditions are not conducive to the project objectives. For example, one gentleman took the posttest directly following having played an intense soccer match with a group of other adult men who are unassociated with any faith tradition. His BSRI score increased significantly for the masculine trait marker. This was surprising since his usual affect is more stereotypically feminine (e.g., more variable emotions, highly sensing and sensitive to others, more relational, etc.). Even so, the soccer player marked the MAAS posttest to show greater mindfulness attention and awareness (0.85). There are a variety of other reasons this particular individual may have scored the BSRI posttest as he did, but are likely not relevant to the present discussion and the scope of this thesis.

Of the four whose BSRI scores increased for the masculine characteristics, two are men. Of the two men, one is the outlier accounted for above. The other began in the androgynous range (-0.5 to 0.5), as did the two women. The move from androgynous to the masculine preference score for these last three was minimal when compared to the outlier. While the BSRI t-test did not show a statistical difference as a result of the intervention a majority already scored in the androgynous range of -0.5—0.5. The overall scores did cluster closer to the androgynous range in the posttest.

Other Factors

All of these factors may call into question the validity and reliability of the measures administered. At the same time, parametric values are usually influenced by trials that are carried out in considerably tighter controlled settings and conditions. Additionally, there is emerging evidence that calls

Results

into question the reproducibility of a significant percentage of published research in Behavioral Science than previously assumed.[3]

One final project design element to consider that likely had some effect on all of the participants, is the regular text sent to their personal cell phones. Regardless of whether or not they attended any or all of the sessions or viewed the LiveStream casts, every participant received the text. Of the three who did not attend or view the sessions, two gave private testimony to the impact the texts personally had on them. These latter two individuals were both experiencing a significant disruption in their lives and described how the prayer message and picture seemed to arrive at an important time in the day. That is, the text helped them to center and pray at moments when they especially needed the reminder to do so. Since their lives were filled with added stress, their increased MAAS scores could be explained by the phone text prompts. Conversely, the improved scores might be due to a Type I error (perceiving an effect that did not actually occur)—if the MAAS score were the DV. That is, the improvement is due to consistent, compassionate attention of the researcher rather than participation in mindfulness practices in the group. There is no indication at present that the non-attenders have any inclination to be a part of group leadership. In contrast, of those who did attend at least some of the group sessions all indicated an eagerness to continue such a program.

The use of cell phone messages and the on-line video component raises another issue concerning variables and research design. The use of digital technology to augment the implementation of the program introduces a third Variable that was not accounted for in the research proposal. There is some evidence that the digital technology had a positive affect on the mindfulness attention and awareness of those who did not attend or view the sessions, shown in the slight increase in posttest MAAS scores. Further, by being a part of smaller groups remotely viewing the sessions rather than in the larger, physical location at the church, the group dynamic is different. Discussion within the remote groups can happen spontaneously while viewing together, uninhibited by the physical presence of the researcher/instructor. Again, with so few participants, meaningful quantitative data is not feasible from which to draw definitive conclusions.

---

3. Open Science Collaboration, "Estimating the Reproducibility of Psychological Science," 6251.

QUALITATIVE DATA

Focus Group Interviews

The focus group that was interviewed before and after the project comprised three project participants. The pre-project focus group described leaders who tend to occupy leadership positions with words that indicate an aggressive posture thirteen times (e.g., "command," "compete," "control," "shape," "aggressive," "demanding," "abusive"). Those who seem to be most successful were described more by their appearance, thirty-two times ("trendy," "tattoo," "hip," "goatee," "flashy," "cool," etc.; and "charismatic," "style," etc.). Successful church leadership was described as operating like a business, ten times ("consumerism," "corporation," importance of "numbers"). Successful churches are generally led by competitive solo leaders (words like, "compare," "cult," "ego," "famous," "infallible," etc.; and "be noticed," "follow," and their "dependents"); even leading by example (e.g., "servant," three times) implied one person showing the way. Good leadership they personally experienced was described more relationally with more compassion-related words ("compassion," "listen," are "vulnerable," and have "wisdom"), and were "empowering" ("enable," "empower," "encourage," "energize," "equip," and are "an example," etc.), the image is still indicative of a solo leader. Examples given were, without exception, male ("he" or "his," etc., used twenty-four times).

In contrast, the post-project focus group interview immediately began defining good leadership as collaborative. Words that describe collaboration were used nineteen times ("in common," "complement each other," "buy-in," "invested," "ownership," "connectedness," share ideas/opinions, "give space" to all, "united"/"unity"). Good leaders were described as seeking the good of all. It was noted that collaborative leadership is more difficult, but not necessarily less efficient since more people take ownership, are invested, and a better decision is made when arrived at together. The "successful" leaders described in the first interview were given the overarching label, "superheroes." When the question concerning structural (cultural/anthropological) meanings that inform underlying themes and contexts, the focus group members seemed to have a better grasp of what the question was asking. One individual indicated that the structure could be described by the sociological designations, "modern" versus "postmodern." It was suggested that the postmodern perspective is more collaborative and reflected most saliently by the computer programming phenomenon, and the corresponding World Wide Web (WWW). Leaders and rulers in modern and pre-modern societies horded information, and when information confers power, those who remain ignorant are also rendered powerless. Assertive, "type-A" personalities, who are controlling and "calling the shots" are rewarded in leadership. And while leadership is mostly male, leaders are increasingly female, yet still were expected to lead in the same manner. After fourteen weeks of mindfulness training for individual practice and as a group, and engaging in group-discernment decision-making, the focus group members see collaborative leadership as the logical, intuitive model for good leadership.

In qualitative research, there is a high risk of tapping into the Hawthorne Effect—the reaction of participants to positively change behavior by virtue of being observed rather than by the intervention itself. In the case of this research design, phenomenological questions are not meant to elicit personal responses, per se (that is, questions that ask the participant to describe personal changes). Rather, the questions are designed to discern whether a shift has occurred in perspective on how leadership is described and what characterizes good or bad leadership. The research questions sought to find whether a shift occurred in participants' understanding of the underlying phenomena involved in how leadership is viewed and the characteristics that are associated with leadership that is perceived as effective. These calculations include which phenomenon determines how we value that which is considered effective. In this case, observed behavior is not a variable, so the Hawthorne Effect is irrelevant. In the cases of individual reports below, the situations were described at random times, unsolicited, and concerning specific accounts of tangible effects of the research program on real-life situations. Again, the Hawthorne Effect is not an issue.

Individual Reports

In addition to the Fitbit-wearing model member, another participant, several weeks into the program recalled a recent conversation with his son. Noticing that he was about to proceed with his habitual style of being only half-present and not fully attentive to his son, the gentleman reflected on this awareness and intentionally centered his attention on his son, initiating an improved relationship between the two. A third project member reported an increasing ability to reflect on his initial, internal responses to stressful situations. Doing so made responding with reasoned reflection—rather than defensive reaction—progressively easier.

The last session focused most of the time on the Group Discernment process. At the DGFUMC site, there were three groups of three to four people. The two LiveStream-only groups each included two members. Each group chose an issue to consider with discernment together. Two of the three DGFUMC groups described very similar conversations around the question of why there are three services, and the style of worship associated with each service. The discussion was very different in each group. One seemed to need more of an understanding and acceptance of why the earliest service continued to be necessary. The other group discussed whether a greater effort was needed to alter the second service to become more distinctly "contemporary." Both groups indicated good communication and productive conversation around taking some sort of action that included at least an active, first step.

For the two LiveStream-only groups, both also communicated that they were better able to understand the issue brought to the discernment process. Both pairs were also able to make a decision that while small was an issue not adequately addressed prior to the program. It is possible that these two groups were able to have more constructive discernment for a couple of reasons. First, each group comprised two leaders from the same place of leadership and with previously understood ministry goals and issues of concern. Second, by attending the sessions remotely, conditions were better for a more focused discussion, as mentioned above.

SIGNIFICANCE OF THE RESULTS

The outcome expected from implementing this project arose from a desire to challenge structural or normative assumptions that underlie leadership practices in the church. To reiterate, it was assumed that developing a theory to describe assumptions attributed to theological bases for the current formation and practice of leadership would enable the theory to be expanded to the *system* of practices. The aim of the project was to allow the experience of participants to inform the church about how group leadership and mindful spiritual practice impact one's perspective of the *other* and of the characteristics ascribed to effective leadership. Where the quantitative data did not support the specific hypothesis supporting the research project, the qualitative data did. Several people described significant effects of mindfulness practices on personal well-being and interpersonal relationships. In addition, the majority of participants described numerous benefits of mindful discernment in group settings for making decisions as leaders in the church. The discussion went as far as making plans to continue teaching and expanding the practice in other areas of the church life and community.

The research also sought to challenge the current practice that reinforces a hierarchy of leadership where one (or few) holds power, as well as leadership that appears monochromic and defines success in terms of quantity of followers (versus peace, justice, unity). Again, the quantitative data did not support with statistical significance a shift in perspective or practice. But, as above, the qualitative results indicated an explicit change in perception of sociological and anthropological influence on common understanding of successful leadership. What is more, specific suggestions and initiation of a plan to extend further extensive change were discussed.

One feature of the research design that made quantifying results elusive was the on-line component. The reasons for including the use of the LiveStream format as part of the research design were twofold. One, given the circumstances of the researcher at the time of the project, the on-line format offered increased possibility for more individuals and groups to participate in the project. Two, there is evidence that emerging generations increasingly use digital technology to communicate, find meaning, and learn.[4] The researcher wished to explore the use of a live stream format with a view to employ the medium for future on-line ministry. In fact, during the project, three participants were ambivalent about actually attending the sessions at the church. Each provided dubious excuses and said that he or she would go ahead and watch the LiveStream cast later that week. Since one Independent Variable depended on a group experience, this blasé attitude toward attending the live session was frustrating and undermined that aspect of the hypothesis.

Still, leadership venues are changing, and the institutional church can no longer rely on a building to *be* the church in the twenty-first century. One of the major issues facing leaders today, and alluded to in chapter 3 above, is the way digital technology is affecting the way young people process information and relate to one another. Indeed, the brains of digital natives (those born in the era when computer technology became ubiquitous

---

4. Jameson, "e-Leadership in Higher Education," 890.

to everyday life—i.e., from about 1995) develop differently than those of digital immigrants (those born before the onset of the dominance of computer technology).[5] Digital natives tend to exhibit more social anxiety and symptoms of Attention Deficit Disorder. At the same time, the technology makes information available to everyone who has a smartphone or personal computer. This fact makes authority, institutional structures, and even the advice of someone older irrelevant—at least, on the surface.

Since authority no longer holds the same sway as it has in generations past, leadership is necessarily shifting in composition and style. Emerging corporations, particularly those that are directly related to computer and web-based enterprises, when they do meet at a physical location, do so in open office space. The open-space office serves two purposes: (1) to facilitate collaboration, and (2) eliminate obvious hierarchical structure. The occupation of computer programming itself is a collaborative endeavor. Just as spoken language mutates and words shift in meaning, new entries appear in the lexicon with increasing frequency, and computer programs are constantly altered. When a computer program is written, countless other programmers add to and change an algorithm here, a command there. No sense of management or hierarchy enters the process except in the case of corporation or business. And, this happens only by the very nature of giving direction to a specific need or product that is being marketed and sold.

The process of recruiting and implementing this research project revealed sufficient evidence that leadership structure and standard practices are dramatically and fundamentally changing. That the BSRI scores of the majority of the participants—pretest and posttest—were in or very near the androgyny range of -0.5 to 0.5 suggests the change is well underway. All of the participants are currently or have been in leadership positions. Yet, all of them identify with and prefer to express androgynous sex-role stereotypes. In other words, none of the participants in this project would naturally lead in a stereotypically masculine mode. This also may be why so many are reluctant to take on a designated leadership role—what is expected is not congruent with the intuitive leadership style.

In addition to the shift in leadership style, very few of the participants demonstrated a sense of obligation to the researcher or the integrity of the research design. That is, a majority seemed to find it acceptable to choose another activity and defer to the LiveStream cast, and not remain

---

5. Draft of the forthcoming book, Mendenhall, "E-Leadership in Social Media," *International Leadership*.

committed to the process to its completion. Even the digital immigrants evidence in varying degrees the short attention spans that digital natives acquire.

Still, another implication this research corroborates concerns the perception of image. The prevalence of smartphone use affects attention span, but it also affects one's sense of identity. Communicating digitally means that communication does not have to be authentic. In fact, image altering is expected, so true identity is lost in translation. The very nature of remote communication precludes the process that happens when iron sharpens iron. Accountability is exceedingly difficult and the type of growth and maturity that face-to-face, real-life relationship naturally produces is thwarted. Sex-role stereotype is less relevant because relationships and work conditions have substantially changed. At the same time, the ability to objectify another is magnified by making one's image digital, changeable, and impersonal. So, while digital technology is changing the way we meet together and lead others, it is also making it much easier to pervert the image of another. And this opens up a whole host of possible addictions and relational issues that is well beyond the scope of this thesis. Future research is suggested in Chapter 6 below.

The fundamental hope by which this research project was advanced was to develop a theory robust enough to motivate action (i.e., practice) to produce healthy people who work together and promote the health and maturity of the whole, while moving in the strength of personal unity with the Triune God—collectively. Specific quantitative data did suggest that physical and interrelational health was improved by participating in group and individual mindfulness practices. Group discernment practices that encourage listening, attention, and awareness of one another was responded to positively. The effect was enough to elicit discussion about ways to continue the practices in other venues and groups associated with the life and structure of the church. Much work is yet to be accomplished, but this is a promising start.

6

Summary

WHAT IS POSSIBLE

THIS PROJECT DEMONSTRATED TO a certain degree that mindfulness practice and group leadership training does impact identification with stereotypic sex role attributes in leadership groups. As we explored with some rigor, Scripture reveals that God is mindful of and speaks directly to humankind. The unique character each person possesses—community, culture, language—expresses God's image. That image is best grasped, then, by knowing and being in relationship with one another. In Christ, all have power to live out God's image, but it is in collaborative, cooperating, love-empowered community that it is more fully expressed.

The Mindfulness Attention Skills Training Group Leadership Program (MAST-GLP) addressed the hypothesis, as mindfulness attention and greater acceptance to members in leadership groups increase, members will identify to a greater degree with androgynous personality characteristics after mindfulness training and group discernment practice. The program was video captured by the LiveStream Producer software while the training was conducted at a suburban Chicago, Illinois, United Methodist church.

Summary

A comprehensive assessment was administered before the start of the program and at its conclusion. The assessment included a measure of mindfulness attention (Mindfulness Attention Awareness Scale), of group cohesiveness (Group Cohesiveness Scale), and identification with stereotypic sex role characteristics (Bem Sex Role Inventory), in addition to demographic information. A pre-project and post-project focus group interview was conducted with three members of the training program. Resources were made available in a Facebook group with links to the LiveStream video of each session, and a link to a Dropbox mp4 files of each video was made available at the end of the training. Every two-to-three days a text message was sent to the phone of each participant as a prompt and word suggestion for centering prayer. Each contained an image associated with a centering word, and a text containing a short prayer focus.

The stated goal of the MAST-GLP was to determine whether mindfulness practice and group leadership training might have an impact on identification with stereotypic sex role attributes in leadership groups. One of the objectives of the program, though, was to challenge a pervasive expectation placed on church leaders to maintain a leadership style that can be described with stereotypically masculine characteristics. While the quantitative data did not definitively show a shift in attitude of participants, the focus group interviews and individual testimonies *did confirm* a change. Participants recognized the advantages for discernment and decision-making as a collaborative, cooperative effort over and against reflexively yielding to the verdict of one person in charge. The post-project reflections demonstrate at the very least, the beginnings of a challenge to structural or normative assumptions that typically drive the leadership practice of deferring to a single leader who seems to be in control of things. There was a general sense each was making space for another to then become empowered to authentically express the self wholly.

Another effect participants of the MAST-GLP noticed relates to a second objective of the program: addressing the diminishing attention and thoughtful reflection that is challenged by a surge in development and prevalence of technological devices, and the lifestyle this technology gives license to. The quantitative instruments showed a slight increase (though not statistical significance) in mindfulness attention and awareness by a majority of the participants. But, it was the individual testimonies and post-session discussions that revealed significant changes in not only the personal lives of each, but also a greater sense of being heard during the group discernment process in the last session. By maintaining greater awareness of one another and the accompanying intergroup trust, individual group members were more likely to contribute to the process and a richer discussion ensued.

Implications of the Research

Since the role of the church is to live out Kingdom of God values characterized by bearing God's image, how the church leads within the church community affects the ways it interacts in the greater community. And the greater community, and society in general, is changing and shifting more rapidly than ever. The church must pay attention and be aware of these changes. The church needs to note how it is viewed by the larger community and reflect an attitude that Paul suggests, to "be all things to all people" (1 Cor 9:22), and Jesus exhorts, to love and be known by love (John 13:34–35). As a church community and as families within that community, it is important for all members to be a part of leading in love.

The reality of the change in societal structure is apparent as Millenials are becoming parents, and doing so with a smartphone in hand. The effects of oversharing images of oneself and one's children are only now being assessed. Still, it is evident that these parents are more stressed by the constant reminders of other parents who portray seemingly perfect parenting. The ever-evolving technology makes communication simple. It is wonderful to be able to share images and thoughts instantly with people who are not near—and even with those who are. The problem is that they are just that: images. And, the technology that develops the photo apps and platforms on which they are shared are increasingly deft. They are easy to use, inexpensive, and alluring. The state of affairs is not new. The advertising industry that began in force in the 1950s exploits those images—people-as-objects of desire—and initiated the damage. Now images can be manipulated with incredible ease with the right tools. Facetune,[1] the latest in photo-editing can whiten teeth, fix stray hairs, delete a pimple, and even make lips fuller and eyes stand out. So, when one can make herself more "perfect" with Facetune, why not have the real thing done surgically? Point in fact, in 2014, 63,538 *teens* opted for cosmetic surgery in the US.[2] With "hashtags"

---

1. Facetune.
2. American Society of Plastic Surgeons, 2014 Plastic Surgeries Report.

Summary

that mark Instagram and Twitter photographs like, #waisttraining, #bikinibridge, and #thighgaps, the extent of the "selfie" impact is self-evident.

Any effort to be countercultural is not easy. To make your true self "face" the public with unaltered face is exponentially onerous. If the church is to be relevant to the community within and outside the wall of the building, addressing what it means to contain a unique aspect of God's character is key. Handheld computers with exceptionally simple apps invite impulsivity effectually rendering reasoned reflection unavailable to the habitual user. The data gathered from the MAST-GDP project and supporting research reveals the impact mindfulness spiritual practices in groups have on pulling down self-erected walls and opening one's eyes to see clearly into an *other*. The data also highlights the enormity of the need and of the task presented the church, or any helping organization. If it is true that mindfulness attention practices can have a significant effect on so many aspects of life (lowered blood pressure and heart rate, decreased anxiety, greater cooperation among group members, etc.), it seems intuitive that intentionally engaging in and teaching these practices in the church or organization is wise and necessary.

The results of the research study hint at the generalizing applicability of this kind of program. As the program participants discussed future possibilities, several mentioned repeating the program as a Sunday school class, but it soon became evident that doing so would merely be slotting in one limited tool for another. Since the research was designed to address structural, normative conventions, the practices need to be integrated into the leadership *infrastructure* in order for the process to make a real impact on the edifice of the church system. The mindfulness practice of prayer deepens the relationship between practitioner and the Spirit of God. By reflecting the character of the *perichoresis*, the spiritual leader participates in the relationship of the Persons of the Trinity and becomes *more than*. Practicing intentional attentiveness as a leadership group increases their capacity to obtain spiritual direction and understanding, and greater courage to enact that direction. There were hints of that courage, but it was clear much more (and consistent) prayer and group discernment practice is necessary.

Possible Future Research

Research findings of this project point to the benefit mindfulness awareness and attention has for unifying the leadership in a church setting. Yet, the project did not show how to effectively integrate a group discernment process into the leadership infrastructure. Pretest BSRI scores indicated that participants were already in or near the androgynous range suggesting a natural progression toward androgynous leadership in general practice. At the same time, more masculine characteristics were used to describe leadership in the pretest data revealing that *expectations of* leaders have not shifted—at least, to the same degree. Further research is needed to tease out the dynamics that describe the reasons behind a general acquiescence to maintain ineffectual or antiquated leadership. Factors that underscore the tendency toward maintaining the status quo and undermine change, particularly as regards expectations of leaders, need further investigation. The fact that a number of social shifts occurred under relatively massive group effort and protest may point the direction for such research. New technology and mobile devices have been used to affect a measure of social gathering around a cause (e.g., the so-called "Arab Spring," "Occupy Wall Street" movement, and "ISIS"), while also being implicated in effecting reduced interpersonal intimacy.

The effect of great human disconnection via changes in technology was recognized during the project and is easily observed in society. When collaboration, discernment, and the values of mindfulness require more human connection, it seems society is sliding even further away from what it needs most. Addressing ways to meet technology with mindfulness practices is worthy of more research. A couple of issues to consider: (1) how to incorporate available technology, and (2) how to discern the effectiveness of technology's tools in creating the space and attention necessary to produce the properties that mindfulness practices are shown to generate.

Since the outcome of this research suggests that being physically present is more necessary than first imagined for cohesion, empathy and collaboration, that quantitative data yielded no statistical significance is not sufficient reason to believe the project itself is ineffectual. Indeed, the qualitative data was promising, as were the conversations with individual participants. Repeating the project over a longer time period (twenty-one weeks versus fourteen weeks) and longer sessions (90–120 minutes versus 60–75 minutes) should yield stronger data. Investigating ways to accomplish this is worth exploring. Another factor to consider is the position

Summary

of the administrator of the project in relationship to the participants. An outsider new to the community may acquire less support. Implementing the project with someone well established and acknowledged as a leader of the group might increase the possibility for greater support and commitment.

What is more, the MAST-GDP revealed the importance of investment and personal commitment of participants to the personal growth process. Research devoted to finding ways to encourage that investment would be useful. Post-project conversations with participants regarding incorporating the program with the church staff meetings unmasked the difficulty of encouraging that commitment. Several individuals remarked that many members of staff would not view it necessary or appropriate to include such practices in meetings. What are some of the reasons for resistance? Is it fear of the practices themselves or the vulnerability mindfulness practice implies? Perhaps, it is an inability to see the value of the personal growth mindfulness is shown to effect, or that it ought to be valued by those leading in such a setting?

One more factor to explore further regards commitment in general. Even of those who finished the course, many did not maintain commitment to the entire process (i.e., attending all of the sessions in person). The aim of the project included *group* discernment. All of the information, materials and personal explanation made this clear. Those who committed to participate in the project via the LiveStream platform did so as a group. Both of these groups met to view the sessions together relatively consistently (one group viewed separately on one occasion; the second group, twice). Of those who agreed to meet at the DGFUMC site, however, more were apt to fall back on the LiveStream option and choose another activity over attending the live session. Again, the problem is multifaceted; emerging technology is a powerful connector and equally effective at thwarting intimacy. So an inquiry into whether our culture is becoming less able to truly enter and sustain direct human interactions is in order. The answer may suggest a calling for the Church.

Possible Routes

Underlying implications of reduced intimacy and accountability, such as inadequate accountability and objectifying images can be addressed and scrutinized in controlled studies. One crucial area regards the use of social media. Interventions, applications and, tech-driven programs need to be objectively evaluated since the potential positive impact on the way social media is used is massive. Social anxiety, distorted body image, and compulsive, inattentive cognition are just a few of the damaging results of unrestrained and unmediated use of social media. The church needs to be part of finding and creating solutions to these issues. As mentioned in chapter 3 above, mindfulness attention and awareness is shown to increase creative thinking. So, if mindfulness is practiced, creative solutions are more likely.

Social media offers a platform for displaying edited pictures of the best (or intended) image of the user. And the message this image is often meant to convey is one of attractiveness. Still more, users offer up the self as object—to be objectified. Once a person becomes an object, perversion is sure to follow. The "real" person cannot be truly known without relationship and usually requires physical proximity. The real challenge, after finding ways to be a subversive presence in social media, is then to insert flesh and blood human beings into the real world schedule and reality of the lives of emerging generations. More research may be able to identify effective means to do so, but it seems the most effective means will be as diverse as the community in which each church finds itself. So, something more of a travelogue-like guide used in the context of group discernment versus a delineation of how-tos, is more apt to be effective.

With regard to leadership style, power differentials are morphing at a greater degree than ever before. There are distinct advantages for each technological innovation, and numerous factors that are negatively impacted. All changes require societal adjustments. For example, in the case of E-mail technology, particularly with the prevalence of smartphones and their notifications, distraction and attention deficit are becoming a force to be reckoned with. At the same time, in the context of business or organizational communication, writing an E-mail gives the space to construct a message versus reflexive responses that can weigh down a deliberation. A benefit to this arrangement is that all involved in the E-mail deliberations maintain a comparatively level power structure. That is, each "voice" is heard in the context of the discussion that may not be noticed in a face-to-face meeting, and makes the in-person meeting more focused and less time-consuming. In this way, social power is reconstructed to be more collaborative and less hierarchical.[3]

---

3. Scholl and Sassenberg, "While You Still Think, I Already Type," 692. See also Jameson, "e-Leadership in Higher Education," 889.

Summary

Additionally, the brains of digital natives—those born in the era when computer technology became ubiquitous to everyday life (i.e., about 1995 and after)—develop differently than those of digital immigrants—born before the onset of the dominance of computer technology. Digital natives tend to exhibit more social anxiety and symptoms of Attention Deficit Disorder. At the same time, the technology makes information available to everyone who has a smartphone or personal computer. This fact makes authority, institutional structures, and *even the advice* of someone older irrelevant—at least, on the surface. More research is required to assess the range of effects digital technology has on the psyche and socialization of emerging generations. Mindfulness practices are shown to address Attention Deficit Disorder and anxiety disorders. The data to support the efficacy of mindfulness attention and awareness are prolific. What is lacking is any plan to meet the need—*in* the reality—with a way to implement mindfulness practices. More apps only provide more options. More options merely increase anxiety and indecision.

Great wisdom and discernment is necessary to intersect the lives of those who possess that wisdom and discernment with those who merely have the information. Digital natives have limitless information at their fingertips, but often lack the wisdom and discernment that comes from experience and reflection. There is a great opportunity for both groups to be mutually beneficial to one another. Humility is the way forward. And, since humility is a disposition that is developed over time, the responsibility lies with the older, wiser group to lead the way.

The church needs to be a creative place that does not seek to control and dictate impersonal dogma if it wants to *be* the message of Jesus in the twenty-first century. Achieving the hope of this project to challenge the current practice that reinforces a hierarchy of leadership where few holds power, as well as leadership that appears monochromic and defines success in terms of quantity rather than peace, justice, and unity is in its beginning. For now, theory has seen a spark of motivation to action to produce healthy people who work together and promote the health and maturity of the whole, while moving in the strength of personal unity with the Triune God—collectively.

Appendix A

ELEMENTS OF THE MAST-GDP

Centering Prayer

"Method Of Centering Prayer"[1]

Breath Prayer

Sometimes we are uncomfortable with silence. Silence can be scary. But, it is often only in the silence that we pay attention: to what is going on with the body, to actual feelings behind behavior, to the voice of God . . . . For Elijah, it was in the "sheer silence," or, "deafening silence" that God's voice could be heard. (1 Kgs 19:11–15)

Two-Minute Drill

Mindfulness is openness to, awareness of things as they are—without judgment. Spiritual discernment in the context of the group is openness to how the Spirit is moving in the situation. Specifically, in the case of this two-minute drill exercise, spiritual discernment happens when each member is open and aware of the Presence, and concerned only with the person whose situation is being held. It is not what *you* would like to say to this person,

---

1. Keating, "Method of Centering Prayer."

Appendix A

or how *you* would personally like the situation to be directed. When you sit in silence—the inner listening—notice what comes to mind—perhaps a verse, a word or phrase to encourage or affirm or direct. When one person shares "noticings," be present to them, hold them loosely (that is, without judgment or thinking ahead to what you want to say).

Group Discernment[2] (group of 5-6 individuals)

- Presenter—2 minutes
  Describe a current or past, personal or ministry situation where you need discernment from God through the group?
    - Silence—2 minutes
- 1st Responder shares "noticings"—2 minutes
    - Silence—2 minuntes
- 2nd Responder shares "noticings"— 2 minutes
    - Silence—2 minuntes
- 3rd Responder shares "noticings"—2 minutes
    - Silence—2 minutes
- [etc. until all member have a chance to respond]
- Presenter's Response—2 minutes

Mindfulness Exercises

Body Scan, Mindfulness of the External World[3]

Befriending the Silence[4]
    Circle of Trust, Touchstones
    "God As Eagle," Imaginative Prayer Exercise.[5]

---

2. Adapted from course notes, Meyer, "Uniting Work and Worship," DMS 818, 2012.
3. Living Well, "Body Scan," "Mindfulness of the External World." http://www.livingwell.org.au
4. Broyles, *Soul Tending*, 38.
5. Oestreicher and Warner, "God As Eagle," 52–53.

APPENDIX A

Circle of Trust

Palmer proposes two major goals for the role of the teacher in such a setting:

1) Creating a space in which there is neither suppression nor concession, but a mutual submission to the bonds of communal truth. The focus is not on instant answers (words, words, words) but rather on adventure, wrestling with untruth, silence, and listening. It is on "hospitality," where everyone is accepted, where one can expose ignorance, express feelings, try out new hypotheses, challenge other ideas, and engage in mutual criticism.

2) Maintaining contact with the transcendent center and love's reality. The study of the "sacred texts" of the discipline (letting the texts speak for themselves), the practice of prayer and meditation, and paying attention to the life of the community itself.[6]

Lectio Divina Bookmark

If you see some brother or sister in need and have the means to do something about it but turn a cold shoulder and do nothing, what happens to God's love? It disappears. And you made it disappear. —1 John 3:17 (The Message)

Lectio Divina

Pray: Loving God, help me hear your word for me. Amen.

Listen: Read the scripture. Write one word or phrase that is important to you in this passage.

Meditate: Write all the ideas that come to mind when you think of the word or phrase.
In silence, read over your list. Think about it.

Pray: Talk with God and listen. Write anything you wish.

Rest: Take a deep breath and rest for a few moments.

---

6. Palmer, *A Hidden Wholeness*, especially chapter 5. Adapted from Parker Palmer's, Circle of Trust groups and retreats, http://www.couragerenewal.org/touchstones/.

Appendix A

Lectio Divina Instruction

Begin by breathing deeply as a way of quieting yourself and opening to the Holy Spirit who is closer to you than your breath. Invite God to speak to you through his Word in these moments.

Keep breathing.

Read passages each time slowly and reflectively, not primarily to gain information or analyze the texts, but listening to get a general idea of the Biblical themes contained in the lectionary Scriptures. *Then choose one passage for reading, pondering and savoring today* using the process of *lectio divina*. You might want to move through a Psalm or Gospel passage, or just a verse or two. *Once you have chosen the passage, read it four times (silently or aloud)* asking a slightly different question each time. Allow for a few moments of silence after each reading.

- In the first reading, listen for the word or the phrase that strikes you. In the silence that follows, just savor the word.

- In the second reading, listen for the way in which your life is touched by this word. What is it in my life that needed to hear this word today?

- In the third reading, listen for an invitation from God contained in this word. Is there something God is inviting me to be, or do in response to this word? What is my response back to God?

- Read the passage a fourth time and rest in the word you have received in total yieldedness and abandonment to the love and the will of God.

- Resolve to "live out" or incarnate the word you have received as God leads.

Visio Divina and Iconography

"Without thinking or feeling some emotion, there is just awareness. There is then no desire for bliss, enlightenment, or to teach others. Things are just as they are. In that so-called emptiness, enjoyment arises of itself. As soon as we try to enjoy, the enjoyment eases. Somehow at the bottom of emptiness (openness, pure awareness), there is enjoyment, fullness, presence and peace."[7]

---

7. Thomas Keating, "Notes from a Deep Conversation," *Contemplative Outreach*, 1.

Appendix A

My grace is enough; it's all you need.
My strength comes into its own in your weakness.
(2 Cor 12:9 [The Message])

Icon of the Madonna[8]
Icon of The Trinity[9]

OnBeing with Krista Tippett[10]

Beannacht

John O'Donohue (http://www.onbeing.org/blog/john-o%27donohue-beannacht/8881)

Posing an Open and Generous Question

Parker Palmer (http://www.onbeing.org/blog/parker-palmer-posing-an-open-and-generous-question/7927)

Just Like Me

Mirabai Bush (http://www.onbeing.org/program/mirabai-bush-search-inside-yourself-contemplation-in-life-and-work/7731)

Body Awareness Movement

Ten-minute Sequence for Mindful Meditation and Movement

Slideshow Instruction (http://www.yogajournal.com/slideshow/10-minute-sequence-to-prepare-for-mindful-meditation/#0)

---

8. Nouwen, *Behold the Beauty of the Lord*, 62.
9. Rublev, "Icon of the Trinity."
10. Tippett, *OnBeing*.

Appendix A

The Examen

In the same manner that you would do a body scan, the Examen is a scan of the day. It is an observation, noticing. (http://pray-as-you-go.org/prayer-resources/the-examen/)

An examen for children, for young adults, for the end of the work week, etc. (http://pray-as-you-go.org/go-deeper/)

Listening to God Together (for the complete protocol, please contact the author)

1. Breathe. Quiet yourself of distractions and open yourself to hear the Spirit.
2. Define the issue that is before you while honoring its complexity. Ask clarifying questions and seek information so to avoid making assumptions.
3. Identify how your life experiences may predispose you to certain outcomes for this issue.
4. Commit to a "holy indifference" to any outcome other than what Jesus might want as he guides you on this issue.

(Carry the wisdom lightly—it may be for step *a*, not through *d*, etc. No longer casting vision, rather, *discover together*—take place *among* the leaders; guide. 3 things happen: Seeing the unimaginable. Sense that God is leading us, not we ourselves. Transformation touches *everyone* in the group—all yielding to the growth of God.

"Listen for the weighty word" (Friends). Keep it simple.[11]

---

11. Adapted from John Anderson, *Group Discernment Protocol*, "Uniting Work and Worship," DMS 818, Denver Seminary, 2012.

Appendix B

ARITFACTS

Sample Picture Texts

Know who you are most truly. You are remarkable. #bewhoyouare #thepaceofgrace #breathe

Appendix B

Sabbath—rest—a broad Space, Presence #bepresent

#LiveFully Breathe life in and #bepresent. Follow with laughter.

Appendix B

#Beloved son, Clark, loves to love on others. He shows me God everyday. You are Beloved. #LoveAndKnow. 1Jn4:7–8

MOBILE DEVICE APPS

- Pray-as-you-go.org
- Centering Prayer
- http://www.loyolapress.com/3minute-retreats-mobile-app.htm
- Ensō | Meditation Timer & Bell
- Headspace
- Living Well (includes 15 mindfulness exercises and 7 relaxation exercises)
- Be Grounded lite is a free app with audio exercises to help you stay in the present when your mind is distracted. Developed by two psychologists.
- Calm—Meditate

Bibliography

Amaro, Ajahn. "Thinking: I. Understanding and Relating to Thought." *Mindfulness* 1 (2010) 189–92.
Ames, Daniel, and Susan Fiske. "Cultural Neuroscience." *Asian Journal of Social Psychology* 13 (2010) 72–85.
American Society of Plastic Surgeons. "2014 Plastic Surgeries Report." (2014) 23. Accessed December 9, 2015. http://www.plasticsurgery.org/Documents/news-resources/statistics/2014-statistics/plastic-surgery-statsitics-full-report.pdf.
Apicella, Coren L., Frank W. Marlowe, James H. Fowler, and Nicholas A. Christakis. "Social Networks and Cooperation in Hunter-Gatherers." *Nature* 481 (2012) 497–501.
Apple Inc. *Dictionary*. *New Oxford American Dictionary*. Oxford, UK: Oxford University Press, Inc., 2013. Retrieved from http://itunes.apple.com.
Areni, Charles S., and Iain Black. "Consumers' Responses to Small Portions: Signaling Increases Savoring and Satiation." *Psychology & Marketing* 32, (2015) 532–43.
Auld, A. Graeme. "Imago Dei in Genesis: Speaking in the Image of God." *Expository Times* 116, (2005) 259–62.
Aupperle, Robin L., Carolyn B. Allard, Erin M. Grimes, Alan N. Simmons, Taru Flagan, Michelle Behrooznia, Shadha H. Cissell, Elizabeth W. Twamley, Steven R. Thorp, Sonya B. Norman, Martin P. Paulus, Murray B. Stein. "Dorsolateral Prefrontal Cortex Activation During Emotional Anticipation and Neuropsychological Performance in Posttraumatic Stress Disorder." *Archives of General Psychiatry* 69 (2012) 11.
Bardi, Anat, and Robin Goodwin. "The Dual Route to Value Change: Individual Processes and Cultural Moderators." *Journal of Cross-Cultural Psychology* 42 (2011) 271–87.
Barton, Ruth Haley. *Pursuing God's Will Together: A Discernment Practice for Leadership Groups*. Downers Grove, IL: IVP Books/Formatio, 2012.
Bauerschmidt, Frederick C. *Julian of Norwich and the Mystical Body Politic of Christ*. Vol. 5. Studies in Spirituality and Theology. Edited by Bernard McGinn, Lawrence Cunningham, and David Tracy. Notre Dame, IN: University of Notre Dame Press, 1999.
Becker, Maja, Vivian L. Vignoles, Ellinor Owe, Rupert Brown, Peter B. Smith, Matt Easterbrook, Ginette Herman, Isabelle de Sauvage, David Bourguignon, Ana

Bibliography

Torres, Leoncio Camino, Flávia Cristina Silveira Lemos, M. Cristina Ferreira, Silvia H. Koller, Roberto González, Diego Carrasco, Maria Paz Cadena, Siugmin Lay, Qian Wang, Michael Harris Bond, Elvia Vargas Trujillo, Paola Balanta, Aune Valk, Kassahun Habtamu Mekonnen, George Nizharadze, Marta Fülöp, Camillo Regalia, Claudia Manzi, Maria Brambilla, Charles Harb, Said Aldhafri, Mariana Martin, Ma Elizabeth J. Macapagal, Aneta Chybicka, Alin Gavreliuc, Johanna Buitendach, Inge Schweiger Gallo, Emre Özgen, Ülkü E. Güner and Nil Yamakoğlu. "Culture and the Distinctiveness Motive: Constructing Identity in Individualistic and Collectivistic Contexts." *Journal of Personality and Social Psychology* 102 (2012) 833–55.

Bem, Sandra L. "Gender Schema Theory: A Cognitive Account of Sex Typing." *Psychological Review* 88 (1981) 354–64.

———. "Gender Schema Theory and Self-Schema Theory Compared: A Comment on Markus, Crane, Bernstein, and Siladi's 'Self-Schemas and Gender.'" *Journal of Personality and Social Psychology* 43 (1982) 1192–94.

Ben-Arieh, Asher, and Muhammad Haj-Yahia. "Corporal Punishment of Children: A Multi-Generational Perspective." *Journal of Family Violence* 23 (2008) 687–95.

Benn, Rita, Tom Akiva, Sari Arel, and Robert W. Roeser. "Mindfulness Training Effects for Parents and Educators of Children with Special Needs." *Developmental Psychology* 48, (2012) 1476–87.

Benson, P., E. Roehlkepartain, and K. Hong. "Spiritual Development." *New Directions For Youth Development* (Summer 2008) 142.

Berger, Anja, and Barbara Krahé. "Negative Attributes Are Gendered Too: Conceptualizing and Measuring Positive and Negative Facets of Sex-Role Identity." *European Journal of Social Psychology* 43 (2013) 516–531.

Bettman, Cathy. "Patriarchy: The Predominant Discourse and Fount of Domestic Violence." *Australian & New Zealand Journal of Family Therapy* 30 (2009) 15–28.

Bird, Phyllis A. "'Male and Female He Created Them': Gen 1:27b in the Context of the Priestly Account of Creation." *Harvard Theological Review* 74 (1981) 129–60.

Boehm, Christopher. "Ancestral Hierarchy and Conflict." *Science* 336 (2012) 844–47.

———. "The Moral Consequences of Social Selection." *Behaviour* 151 (2014) 167–83.

Bowlby, John. "Attachment Theory and Its Therapeutic Implications." *Adolescent Psychiatry* 6 (1978) 5–33.

———. *A Secure Base: Parent-Child Attachment and Healthy Human Development*. New York: Basic Books, 1988.

Boyle, Gregory J. "Myers-Briggs Type Indicator (MBTI): Some Psychometric Limitations." *Australian Psychologist* 30 (1995) 71–74.

Brewer, Judson A., Hani M. Elwafi, and Jake H. Davis. "Craving to Quit: Psychological Models and Neurobiological Mechanisms of Mindfulness Training as Treatment for Addictions." *Translational Issues in Psychological Science* 1 (2014) 70–90.

Briggs, Richard S. "Humans in the Image of God and Other Things Genesis Does Not Make Clear." *Journal of Theological Interpretation* 4 (2010) 111–26.

Broderick, Patricia C., and Patricia A. Jennings. "Mindfulness for Adolescents: A Promising Approach to Supporting Emotion Regulation and Preventing Risky Behavior." *New Directions for Youth Development* 136 (2012) 111–26.

Brown, Kirk W., and Richard M. Ryan. "The Benefits of Being Present: Mindfulness and Its Role in Psychological Well-Being." *Journal of Personality and Social Psychology* 84 (2003) 24.

Bibliography

Brown, Kirk Warren, Richard M. Ryan, Tamara M. Loverich, Gina M. Biegel, and Angela Marie West. "Out of the Armchair and into the Streets: Measuring Mindfulness Advances Knowledge and Improves Interventions: Reply to Grossman." *Psychological Assessment* 23 (2011) 1041–46.

Brown, Kirk Warren, and Tim Kasser. "Are Psychological and Ecological Well-Being Compatible? The Role of Values, Mindfulness, and Lifestyle." *Social Indicators Research* 74 (2005) 349–68.

Broyles, Anne. *Soul Tending: Life-Forming Practices for Older Youth and Young Adults.* Nashville, TN: Abingdon, 2002.

Brueggemann, Walter. *The Message of the Psalms: A Theological Commentary.* Augsburg Old Testament Studies. Minneapolis: Augsburg, 1984.

Buñuel, Luis. *My Last Breath.* Translated by Abigail Israel. London: Collins Publishing Group, 1985.

Burch, Vidyamala, and Danny Penman. *You Are Not Your Pain: Using Mindfulness to Relieve Pain, Reduce Stress, and Restore Well-Being—An Eight-Week Program.* New York: Flatiron Books, 2015.

Buss, David M. "The Psychology of Human Mate Selection: Exploring the Complexity of the Strategic Repertoire." In *Handbook of Evolutionary Psychology: Ideas, Issues, and Applications,* edited by Charles B. Crawford and Dennis L. Krebs, 405–29. Mahwah, NJ: Lawrence Erlbaum Associates, 1998.

Byassee, Jason. "Closer Than Kissing: Sarah Coakley's Early Work." *Anglican Theological Review* 90 (2008) 139–55.

Cacioppo, Stephanie, John P. Capitanio, and John T. Cacioppo. "Toward a Neurology of Loneliness." *Psychological Bulletin Psychological Bulletin* (2014).

Campbell, Douglas A., and Alan J. Torrance. *Gospel and Gender: A Trinitarian Engagement with Being Male and Female in Christ.* Studies in Theology and Sexuality. New York: T&T Clark International, 2003.

Carlson, Linda E., and Kirk Warren Brown. "Validation of the Mindful Attention Awareness Scale in a Cancer Population." *Journal of Psychosomatic Research* 58 (2005) 29–33.

Carmody, James, Ruth A. Baer, Emily L. B. Lykins, and Nicholas Olendzki. "An Empirical Study of the Mechanisms of Mindfulness in a Mindfulness-Based Stress Reduction Program." *Journal of Clinical Psychology* 65 (2009) 613–26.

Charleton, James. *Non-Dualism in Eckhart, Julian of Norwich and Traherne: A Theopoetic Reflection.* New York: Bloomsbury Academic, 2013.

Childs, Brevard Springs. "Speech-Act Theory and Biblical Interpretation." *Scottish Journal of Theology* 58 (2005) 375–92.

Chow, Rey. "'I Insist on the Christian Dimension': On Forgiveness . . . And the Outside of the Human." *Differences: A Journal of Feminist Cultural Studies* 20 (2009) 224–49.

Coakley, Sarah. "Evolution, Cooperation, and Divine Providence." In *Evolution, Games, and God: The Principle of Cooperation,* edited by Martin A. Nowak and Sarah Coakley, 375–85. Cambridge, MA: Harvard University Press, 2013.

———. "Introduction: Disputed Questions in Patristic Trinitarianism." *Harvard Theological Review* 100 (2007) 125–38.

———. *Powers and Submissions: Spirituality, Philosophy, and Gender* Challenges in Contemporary Theology. Malden, MA: Blackwell, 2002.

Bibliography

———. "Prayer, Politics and the Trinity: Vying Models of Authority in Third-Fourth-Century Debates on Prayer and 'Orthodoxy.'" *Scottish Journal of Theology* 66 (2013) 379–99.

———. "Re-Thinking Gregory of Nyssa: Introduction—Gender, Trinitarian Analogies, and the Pedagogy of the Song." *Modern Theology* 18 (2002) 431–43.

Coatsworth, J. Douglas, Larissa G. Duncan, Robert L. Nix, Mark T. Greenberg, Jochebed G. Gayles, Katharine T. Bamberger, Elaine Berrena, and Mary Ann Demi. "Integrating Mindfulness with Parent Training: Effects of the Mindfulness-Enhanced Strengthening Families Program." *Developmental Psychology* 51 (2015) 26–35.

Cobb, L. Stephanie. *Dying to Be Men: Gender and Language in Early Christian Martyr Texts*. Gender, Theory, and Religion. New York: Columbia University Press, 2008.

Cohen, Jacob. "A Power Primer." *Psychological Bulletin* 112 (1992) 155–59.

Colin, James. "Law Student Wellbeing: Benefits of Promoting Psychological Literacy and Self-Awareness Using Mindfulness, Strengths Theory and Emotional Intelligence." *Legal Education Review* 21 (2011) 217–33. https://www.academia.edu/8275714/Law_Student_Wellbeing_Benefits_of_Promoting_Psychological_Literacy_and_Self-Awareness_Using_Mindfulness_Strengths_Theory_and_Emotional_Intelligence.

Collins, Jim. *Good to Great and the Social Sectors*. San Francisco: Harper, 2005.

Cone, John, and Sharon Foster. *Dissertations and Theses: From Start to Finish*. 2nd ed. Washington, DC: American Psychological Association, 2010.

Conway, Colleen M. "Dying to Be Men: Gender and Language in Early Christian Martyr Texts." *Church History* 78 (2009) 873–75.

Cotterill, Sarah, James Sidanius, Arjun Bhardwaj, and Vivek Kumar. "Ideological Support for the Indian Caste System: Social Dominance Orientation, Right-Wing Authoritarianism and Karma." *Journal of Social and Political Psychology* 2 (2014) 554–70.

Creswell, John W. *Qualitative Inquiry & Research Design: Choosing among Five Approaches*. Thousand Oaks, CA: Sage, 2007.

Daneshjoo, Mohammad Bagher, Shokouh Navabinejad, and Abdollah Shfia-Abadi. "Comparing Effectiveness of Schema Therapy and Mindfulness-Based Relapse Prevention (MBRP) in Resiliency of Drug Addicts in Shiraz Addiction Clinics." *International Journal of Academic Research* 7 (2015): 575–78.

Davies, Martin Brett. *Doing a Successful Research Project: Using Qualitative or Quantitative Methods*. New York: Palgrave Macmillan 2007.

Dawes, Christopher T., James H. Fowler, Tim Johnson, Richard McElreath, and Oleg Smirnov. "Egalitarian Motives in Humans." *Nature* 446 (2007) 794–96.

Dean, Kenda Creasy, and Ron Foster. *The Godbearing Life: The Art of Soul Tending for Youth Ministry*. Nashville, TN: Upper Room Books, 1998.

Delcore, Henry D. "New Reflections on Old Questions in the Anthropology of Gender." *Reviews in Anthropology* 36 (2007) 109–30.

DePree, Max. *Leadership Is an Art*. New York: Currency, 2004.

Donaldson, Stewart I., and Elisa J. Grant-Vallone. "Understanding Self-Report Bias in Organizational Behavior Research." *Journal of Business and Psychology* 17 (2002) 245–60.

Donnan, Hastings, and Fiona Magowan. *The Anthropology of Sex*. Oxford, UK: Berg, 2010.

Dube Shomanah, Musa W. *Postcolonial Feminist Interpretation of the Bible*. St. Louis, MO: Chalice Press, 2000.

Bibliography

Duguid, Michelle M., and Melissa C. Thomas-Hunt. "Condoning Stereotyping? How Awareness of Stereotyping Prevalence Impacts Expression of Stereotypes." *Journal of Applied Psychology* 100 (2015) 343–59.

Dy-Liacco, Gabriel S., M. Christine Kennedy, Donna J. Parker, and Ralph L. Piedmont. "Spiritual Transcendence as an Unmediated Causal Predictor of Psychological Growth and Worldview among Filipinos." *Research in the Social Scientific Study of Religion* 16 (2005) 25.

Eagly, Alice H., and Wendy Wood. "Sexual Selection Does Not Provide an Adequate Theory of Sex Differences in Aggression." *Behavioral and Brain Sciences* 32 (2009) 276–77.

Echabe, Agustin Echebarria. "Role Identities Versus Social Identities: Masculinity, Femininity, Instrumentality and Communality." *Asian Journal of Social Psychology* 13 (2010) 30.

Ellison, Christopher G., and Matt Bradshaw. "Religious Beliefs, Sociopolitical Ideology, and Attitudes toward Corporal Punishment." *Journal of Family Issues* 30 (2009) 320–40.

Elwafi, Hani M., Katie Witkiewitz, Sarah Mallik, Thomas A. Thornhill IV, and Judson A. Brewer. "Mindfulness Training for Smoking Cessation: Moderation of the Relationship between Craving and Cigarette Use." *Drug & Alcohol Dependence* 130 (2013) 222–29.

"The Emancipation Proclamation," U.S. National Archives & Records Administration. (2015) www.archives.gov/exhibits/featured_documents/emancipation_proclamation.

Ember, Carol, Teferi Adem, and Ian Skoggard. "Risk, Uncertainty, and Violence in Eastern Africa." *Human Nature* 24 (2013) 33–58.

Emerson, Katherine T. U., and Mary C. Murphy. "Identity Threat at Work: How Social Identity Threat and Situational Cues Contribute to Racial and Ethnic Disparities in the Workplace." *Cultural Diversity and Ethnic Minority Psychology* 20 (2014) 508–20.

EnginDeniz, M., Alkım Arı, Seher Akdeniz and Hatice İrem Özteke. "The Prediction of Decision Self-Esteem and Decision Making Styles by Mindfulness." *International Online Journal of Educational Sciences* 7 (2015) 45–50. www.iojes.net//userfiles/Article/IOJES_1194.pdf.

England, John C. *Northeast Asia*. Vol. 3 of *Asian Christian Theologies: A Research Guide to Authors, Movements, Sources*. Maryknoll, NY: Orbis, 2004.

Entwistle, David N., and Stephen K. Moroney. "Integrative Perspectives on Human Flourishing: The Imago Dei and Positive Psychology." *Journal of Psychology & Theology* 39 (2011) 295–303.

Epel, Elissa, Jennifer Daubenmier, Judith Tedlie Moskowitz, Susan Folkman, and Elizabeth Blackburn. "Can Meditation Slow Rate of Cellular Aging? Cognitive Stress, Mindfulness, and Telomeres." In *Longevity, Regeneration, and Optimal Health: Integrating Eastern and Western Perspectives*, edited by William C. Bushell, Erin L. Olivo and Neil D. Theise, 34–53. Boston: Wiley-Blackwell, 2009.

Everding, H. Edward, Clarence H. Snelling Jr., and Mary M. Wilcox. "A Shaping Vision of Community for Teaching in an Individualistic World: Ephesians 4:1–16 and Developmental Interpretation." *Religious Education* 83 (1988) 423–37.

"Facetune." Lightricks, Ltd. Last modified 2014. http://www.facetuneapp.com/.

Fergusson, David. "Humans Created According to the Imago Dei: An Alternative Proposal." *Zygon* 48 (2013) 439–53.

Bibliography

Fetters, Michael D., Leslie A. Curry, and John W. Creswell. "Achieving Integration in Mixed Methods Designs-Principles and Practices." *Health Services Research* 48 (2013) 2134–56.

Franzen, Aaron. "Reading the Bible in America: The Moral and Political Attitude Effect." *Review of Religious Research* 55 (2013) 19.

Friedman, Stacey R., and Carol S. Weissbrod. "Attitudes Toward the Continuation of Family Rituals among Emerging Adults." *Sex Roles* 50 (2004) 277–84.

Frymer-Kensky, Tikva Simone. *Reading the Women of the Bible*. New York: Schocken Books, 2002.

Fu, Feng, and Martin Nowak. "Global Migration Can Lead to Stronger Spatial Selection Than Local Migration." *Journal of Statistical Physics* 151 (2013) 637–653.

Fuchs, Rüdiger. "I Kneel before the Father and Pray for You (Ephesians 3:14): Date and Significance of Ephesians, Part 1." *European Journal of Theology* 23 (2014) 13–22.

Fuentes, Agustín. "A New Synthesis: Resituating Approaches to the Evolution of Human Behaviour." *Anthropology Today* 25 (2009) 12–17.

Fukuyama, Francis. "What Is Governance?" *Governance* 26 (2013) 347–68.

Gino, Francesca, and Sreedhari D. Desai. "Memory Lane and Morality: How Childhood Memories Promote Prosocial Behavior." *Journal of Personality and Social Psychology* 102 (2012) 743–58.

Gladd, Benjamin L. "The Last Adam as the 'Life-Giving Spirit' Revisited: A Possible Old Testament Background of One of Paul's Most Perplexing Phrases." *Westminster Theological Journal* 71 (2009) 297–309.

Goldberg, Dave, and Selina Tobaccowala, "Surveymonkey" (2015). www.surveymonkey.com/mp/take-a-tour/?ut_source=header.

Goldberg, Simon B., James M. Davis, and William T. Hoyt. "The Role of Therapeutic Alliance in Mindfulness Interventions: Therapeutic Alliance in Mindfulness Training for Smokers." *Journal of Clinical Psychology* 69 (2013) 936–50.

Goldberg, Steven. "Why Patriarchy?" *Group* 32 (2008) 13–21.

Goodwin, Doug. "Obsessed with Governance." *Touchstone* 31 (2013) 36–46.

Granados Rojas, Juan Manuel. "Ephesians 4,12: A Revised Reading." *Biblica* 92 (2011) 81–96.

Greenaway, Katharine H., S. Alexander Haslam, Tegan Cruwys, Nyla R. Branscombe, Renate Ysseldyk, and Courtney Heldreth. "From 'We' to 'Me': Group Identification Enhances Perceived Personal Control with Consequences for Health and Well-Being." *Journal of Personality and Social Psychology* (May 2015) 1–18.

Greenfield, Patricia M. "Linking Social Change and Developmental Change: Shifting Pathways of Human Development." *Developmental Psychology* 45 (2009) 18.

Grenz, Stanley J. *The Social God and the Relational Self: A Trinitarian Theology of the Imago Dei*. Louisville, KY: Westminster John Knox Press, 2001.

———. *Theology for the Community of God*. Grand Rapids, MI: Eerdmans, 2000.

Gudbergsen, Thomas. "God Consists of Both the Male and the Female Genders: A Short Note on Gen 1:27." *Vetus testamentum* 62 (2012) 450–53.

Gunton, Colin E. *Act & Being: Toward a Theology of the Divine Attributes*. Grand Rapids, MI: Eerdmans, 2003.

Haas, Alan S., and Ellen J. Langer. "Mindful Attraction and Synchronization: Mindfulness and Regulation of Interpersonal Synchronicity." *NeuroQuantology* 12 (2014) 21–34.

Hamman, Jaco J. "Resistance to Women in Ministry and the Psychodynamics of Sadness." *Pastoral Psychology* 59 (2010) 769–81.

Bibliography

Harader, Joanna. "Holy Spaces of Inclusion: Reflections on the MCUSA Convention 2013, Phoenix." *Mennonite Life (Online)* 68 (2014).

Harrelson, W. J. *The New Interpreter's Study Bible: New Revised Standard Version with the Apocrypha*. Nashville, TN: Abingdon, 2003.

Harris, John L. "An Exposition of Genesis 2:4–11:32." *Southwestern Journal of Theology* 44 (2001) 39–55.

Hart, Rona, Itai Ivtzan, and Dan Hart. "Mind the Gap in Mindfulness Research: A Comparative Account of the Leading Schools of Thought." *Review of General Psychology* 17 (2013) 453–66.

Harvie, Timothy. "Living the Future: The Kingdom of God in the Theologies of Jürgen Moltmann and Wolfhart Pannenberg." *International Journal of Systematic Theology* 10 (2008) 149–64.

Heberle, A. E., and A. S. Carter. "Cognitive Aspects of Young Children's Experience of Economic Disadvantage." *Psychological Bulletin* 141 (2015) 723–46.

Herring, Stephen L. "A 'Transubstantiated' Humanity: The Relationship between the Divine Image and the Presence of God in Genesis I 26f." *Vetus testamentum* 58 (2008) 480–94.

Hofstede, Geert. *Masculinity and Femininity: The Taboo Dimension of National Cultures*. Cross-Cultural Psychology Series, vol. 3. Thousand Oaks, CA: Sage, 1998.

Hudson, Nathan W., and R. Chris Fraley. "Volitional Personality Trait Change: Can People Choose to Change Their Personality Traits?" *Journal of Personality and Social Psychology* 109 (2015) 490–507.

Hülsheger, Ute R., Jonas W. B. Lang, Franziska Depenbrock, Carmen Fehrmann, Fred R. H. Zijlstra, and Hugo J. E. M. Alberts. "The Power of Presence: The Role of Mindfulness at Work for Daily Levels and Change Trajectories of Psychological Detachment and Sleep Quality." *Journal of Applied Psychology* 99 (2014) 1113–28.

Imperatori-Lee, Natalia. "Special Section: Catholic Feminism." *Journal of Feminist Studies in Religion* 31 (Fall 2015) 89–107.

"International Alliance of Women for Suffrage and Legal Citizenship." *International Alliance of Women* (2015). http://womenalliance.org/what-is-iaw.

International Leadership: A Reference Guide. Edited by Mark E. Mendenhall. Santa Barbara, CA: Mission Bell Media, 2016.

James, Colin. "Law Student Wellbeing: Benefits of Promoting Psychological Literacy and Self-Awareness Using Mindfulness, Strengths Theory and Emotional Intelligence." *Legal Education Review* 21 (2011). http://heinonline.org.

Jameson, Jill. "E-Leadership in Higher Education: The Fifth 'Age' of Educational Technology Research." *British Journal of Educational Technology* 44 (2013).

Janssens, Heleen, Maykel Verkuyten, and Aqeel Khan. "Perceived Social Structural Relations and Group Stereotypes: A Test of the Stereotype Content Model in Malaysia." *Asian Journal of Social Psychology* 18 (2015) 52–61.

Jantzen, Grace. *Julian of Norwich: Mystic and Theologian*. Mahwah, NJ: Paulist Press, 2000.

Jensen, Eric. *Teaching with the Brain in Mind*. 2nd ed. Alexandria, VA: Association for Supervision and Curriculum Development, 2005.

Jensen, Frances E., and Amy Ellis Nutt. *The Teenage Brain: A Neuroscientist's Survival Guide to Raising Adolescents and Young Adults*. New York: Harper, 2014.

Jiménez, Manuel, Raúl Aguilar, and José R. Alvero-Cruz. "Effects of Victory and Defeat on Testosterone and Cortisol Response to Competition: Evidence for Same Response Patterns in Men and Women." *Psychoneuroendocrinology* 37 (2012) 1577–81.

Bibliography

Jislin-Goldberg, Tamar, Galia Tanay, and Amit Bernstein. "Mindfulness and Positive Affect: Cross-Sectional, Prospective Intervention, and Real-Time Relations." *The Journal of Positive Psychology* 7 (2012) 349–61.

Jordan, Jillian J., David G. Rand, Samuel Arbesman, James H. Fowler, and Nicholas A. Christakis. "Contagion of Cooperation in Static and Fluid Social Networks." *PLoS ONE* 8 (2013) 1–10.

Jordan-Young, Rebecca, and Raffaella I. Rumiati. "Hardwired for Sexism? Approaches to Sex/Gender in Neuroscience." *Neuroethics* 5 (2012) 305–15.

Kabat-Zinn, Jon. "Mindfulness-Based Interventions in Medicine and Psychiatry: What Does It Mean to Be 'Mindfulness-Based'?" In *The Healing Power of Meditation: Leading Experts on Buddhism, Psychology, and Medicine Explore the Health Benefits of Contemplative Practice*, edited by Andy Fraser, 93–119. Boston: Shambhala, 2013.

Kaplan, Jonathan S. *Urban Mindfulness: Cultivating Peace, Presence & Purpose in the Middle of It All*. Oakland, CA: New Harbinger, 2010.

Kartzow, Marianne Bjelland. "'Asking the Other Question': An Intersectional Approach to Galatians 3:28 and the Colossian Household Codes." *Biblical Interpretation* 18 (2010) 364–89.

Keating, Thomas. "Notes from a Deep Conversation." *Contemplative Outreach: Silence, Solitude, Solidarity, Service—News* 31 (2015).

———. "Method of Centering Prayer." Contermplative Outreach, Ltd., http://www.contemplativeoutreach.org/

Kent, Russell L., and Sherry E. Moss. "Effects of Sex and Gender Role on Leader Emergence." *Academy of Management Journal* 37 (1994) 1335–46.

Khoury-Kassabri, Mona. "Attitudes of Arab and Jewish Mothers Towards Punitive and Non-Punitive Discipline Methods." *Child & Family Social Work* 15 (2010) 135–44.

Kilby, Karen. "Is an Apophatic Trinitarianism Possible?" *International Journal of Systematic Theology* 12 (2010) 65–77.

———. "Too Many Trinities? Kendall Soulen's Trinitarian Trinitarianism." *Pro Ecclesia* 23 (2014) 28–32.

Kim, Hyunji, Ulrich Schimmack, and Shigehiro Oishi. "Cultural Differences in Self- and Other-Evaluations and Well-Being: A Study of European and Asian Canadians." *Journal of Personality and Social Psychology* 102 (2012) 856–73.

Knauft, Bruce M. "Violence and Sociality in Human Evolution." *Current Anthropology* 32 (1991) 391–428.

Koenig, Anne M., Alice H. Eagly, Abigail A. Mitchell, and Tiina Ristikari. "Are Leader Stereotypes Masculine? A Meta-Analysis of Three Research Paradigms." *Psychological Bulletin* 137 (2011) 616–42.

Kuan, Jeffrey K., and Mai-Anh Le Tran. "Reading Race Reading Rahab: A 'Broad' Asian American Reading of a 'Broad' Other." In *Postcolonial Interventions*, edited by Tat-siong Benny Liew, 27–44. Sheffield, UK: Sheffield, 2009.

Kumar, Ranjit. *Research Methodology: A Step by Step Guide for Beginners*. Thousand Oaks, CA: Sage, 2010.

Kwok, Pui-lan. *Postcolonial Imagination and Feminist Theology*. Louisville, KY: Westminster John Knox, 2005.

LaCugna, Catherine Mowry. *God for Us: The Trinity and Christian Life*. San Francisco: HarperSanFrancisco, 1991.

Lai, Pan-Chiu. "Sino-Theology, the Bible and the Christian Tradition." *Studies in World Christianity* 12 (2006) 266–81.

Bibliography

Lao-Tzu. *The Tao-Te Ching*. Vol. 39. Sacred Books of the East, 1891 (2014). http://classics.mit.edu/Lao/taote.1.1.html.

Layoun, Mary N. *Wedded to the Land? Gender, Boundaries, and Nationalism in Crisis Post-Contemporary Interventions*. Durham, NC: Duke University Press, 2001.

Lee, Sang Hyun. *From a Liminal Place: An Asian American Theology*. Minneapolis, Minn: Fortress, 2010.

Lefebvre, Henri. *The Production of Space*. Translated by Donald Nicholson-Smith. Malden, MA: Blackwell, 1991.

Lester, Stan. "An Introduction to Phenomenological Research." (1999). www.sld.demon.co.uk/resmethy.pdf.

Libby, Daniel J., Patrick D. Worhunsky, Corey E. Pilver, and Judson A. Brewer. "Meditation-Induced Changes in High-Frequency Heart Rate Variability Predict Smoking Outcomes." *Frontiers in Human Neuroscience* 6 (2012).

Living Well. "Mindfulness Exercises." *Well Being* (2016) http://www.livingwell.org.au.

Lo, Lung-kwong. "'Neither Jew nor Greek': Galatians 3:28 Revisited." *Annali di storia dell'esegesi* 27 (2010) 25–33.

Lynch, Martin F., Jennifer G. La Guardia, and Richard M. Ryan. "On Being Yourself in Different Cultures: Ideal and Actual Self-Concept, Autonomy Support, and Well-Being in China, Russia, and the United States." *The Journal of Positive Psychology* 4 (2009) 14.

Mackie, Scott D. "Confession of the Son of God in the Exordium of Hebrews." *Journal for the Study of the New Testament* 30 (2008) 437–53.

MacLeod, David J. "The Finality of Christ: An Exposition of Hebrews 1:1–4." *Bibliotheca sacra* 162 (2005) 210–30.

Marks, Loren. "Sacred Practices in Highly Religious Families: Christian, Jewish, Mormon, and Muslim Perspectives." *Family Process* 43 (2004) 217–31.

Marler, Joan. "The Myth of Universal Patriarchy: A Critical Response to Cynthia Eller's Myth of Matriarchal Prehistory." *Feminist Theology: The Journal of the Britain & Ireland School of Feminist Theology* 14 (2006) 163–87.

Marmarosh, Cheri, Ari Holtz, and Michele Schottenbauer. "Group Cohesiveness, Group-Derived Collective Self-Esteem, Group-Derived Hope, and the Well-Being of Group Therapy Members." *Group Dynamics: Theory, Research, and Practice* 9 (2005) 32–44.

Marturano, Antonio. *International Leadership: A Reference Guide*. Edited by Mark E. Mendenhall. Santa Barbara, CA: Mission Bell Media, 2016.

McCarthy, Barry, and Lana M. Wald. "Mindfulness and Good Enough Sex." *Sexual & Relationship Therapy* 28 (2013) 39–47.

McFadyen, Alistair. "Imaging God: A Theological Answer to the Anthropological Question?" *Zygon: Journal of Religion & Science* 47 (2012) 918–33.

McKay, Brad, Gabriele Wulf, Rebecca Lewthwaite, and Andrew Nordin. "The Self: Your Own Worst Enemy? A Test of the Self-Invoking Trigger Hypothesis." *The Quarterly Journal of Experimental Psychology* 68 (2015) 1–10.

Meyer, Keith. *Whole Life Transformation: Becoming the Change Your Church Needs*. Downers Grove, IL: InterVarsity, 2010.

Miller, Jonas G., Sarah Kahle, Monica Lopez, and Paul D. Hastings. "Compassionate Love Buffers Stress-Reactive Mothers from Fight-or-Flight Parenting." *Developmental Psychology* 51 (2015) 36–43.

Moltmann, Jürgen. *Sun of Righteousness, Arise! God's Future for Humanity and the Earth*. Minneapolis: Fortress, 2010.

Bibliography

Morse, MaryKate. *Making Room for Leadership: Power, Space and Influence*. Downers Grove, IL: InterVarsity, 2008.

Murphy, Megan J., Liza C. Mermelstein, Katie M. Edwards, and Christine A. Gidycz. "The Benefits of Dispositional Mindfulness in Physical Health: A Longitudinal Study of Female College Students." *Journal of American College Health* 60 (2012) 341–48.

Nelson, Michelle R., Frédéric F. Brunel, Magne Supphellen, and Rajesh V. Manchanda. "Effects of Culture, Gender, and Moral Obligations on Responses to Charity Advertising across Masculine and Feminine Cultures." *Journal of Consumer Psychology (Lawrence Erlbaum Associates)* 16 (2006) 45–56.

Neuburger, Sarah, Petra Jansen, Martin Heil, and Claudia Quaiser-Pohl. "A Threat in the Classroom: Gender Stereotype Activation and Mental-Rotation Performance in Elementary-School Children." *Journal of Psychology* 220 (2012) 61–69.

Nielsen, Eduard. "Creation and the Fall of Man: A Cross-Disciplinary Investigation." *Hebrew Union College Annual* 43 (1972) 1–22.

Nilsson, Håkan. "A Four-Dimensional Model of Mindfulness and Its Implications for Health." *Psychology of Religion and Spirituality* 6 (2014) 162–74.

Niskanen, Paul. "The Poetics of Adam: The Creation of אדם in the Image of אלהים." *Journal of Biblical Literature* 128 (2009) 417–36.

The Northumbria Community Trust, Ltd. *Celtic Daily Prayer: Prayers and Readings from the Northumbria Community*. New York: HarperOne, 2002.

Nouwen, Henri J. M. *Behold the Beauty of the Lord: Praying with Icons*. Notre Dame, IN: Ave Maria Press, 2007.

Nowak, Martin A. "Five Rules for the Evolution of Cooperation." *Science* 314 (2006) 1560–63.

Nowak, Martin A., and Sarah Coakley. *Evolution, Games, and God: The Principle of Cooperation*. Cambridge, MA: Harvard University Press, 2013.

Oden, Thomas C. *Systematic Theology, Vol 3: Life in the Spirit*. New York: HarperCollins, 1992.

Oestreicher, Jeannie, and Larry Warner. *Imaginative Prayer for Youth Ministry*. Grand Rapids, MI: Zondervan, 2006.

Oliveira, Rui F., and Gonçalo A. Oliveira. "Androgen Modulation of Social Decision Making Mechanisms in the Brain: An Integrative and Embodied Perspective." *Frontiers in Neuroscience* 8 (2014).

Open Science Collaboration. "Estimating the Reproducibility of Psychological Science." *Science* 349 (2015).

Oswald, Patricia A. "An Examination of the Current Usefulness of the Bem Sex-Role Inventory." *Psychological Reports* 94 (2004) 1331–36.

Ozawa-DeSilva, Chikako, and Brenda Ozawa-DeSilva. "Secularizing Religious Practices: A Study of Subjectivity and Existential Transformation in Naikan Therapy." *Journal for the Scientific Study of Religion* 49 (2010) 147–61.

Palmer, Parker. *A Hidden Wholeness: The Journey toward an Undivided Life*. San Francisco: Jossey-Bass, 2004.

———. Circle of Trust: Groups and Retreats, http://www.couragerenewal.org/touchstones/.

Pannenberg, Wolfhart. *Anthropology in Theological Perspective*. Philadelphia: Westminster, 1985.

Bibliography

Parent, Mike C., Bonnie Moradi, Christina M. Rummell, and David M. Tokar. "Evidence of Construct Distinctiveness for Conformity to Masculine Norms." *Psychology of Men & Masculinity* 12 (2011) 354–67.
Parent, Mike C., and Andrew P. Smiler. "Metric Invariance of the Conformity to Masculine Norms Inventory-46 among Women and Men." *Psychology of Men & Masculinity* 14 (2013) 324–28.
Peters, Ted. *God as Trinity: Relationality and Temporality in Divine Life*. Louisville, KY: Westminster/John Knox, 1993.
Phan, Peter C. *The Cambridge Companion to the Trinity*. Cambridge Companions to Religion. New York: Cambridge University Press, 2011.
Rah, Soong-Chan. *The Next Evangelicalism: Freeing the Church from Western Cultural Captivity*. Downers Grove, IL: Intervarsity, 2009.
Rampley, Matthew. "Bildwissenschaft: Theories of the Image in German-Language Scholarship." In *Art History and Visual Studies in Europe: Transnational Discourses and National Frameworks*, edited by Matthew Rampley, Thierry Lenain, Hubert Locher, Andrea Pinotti, Charlotte Schoell-Glass, and Kitty Zijlmans, 119–34. Boston: Brill, 2012.
Rand, David G., Anna Dreber, Omar S. Haque, Rob J. Kane, Martin A. Nowak, and Sarah Coakley. "Religious Motivations for Cooperation: An Experimental Investigation Using Explicit Primes." *Religion, Brain & Behavior* 4 (2013) 31–48.
Reinhard, Kathryn L. "Joy to the Father, Bliss to the Son: Unity and the Motherhood Theology of Julian of Norwich." *Anglican Theological Review* 89, no. 4 (2007): 629–645.
Reiss, Moshe. "Adam: Created in the Image and Likeness of God." *Jewish Bible Quarterly* 39 (2011) 181–86.
Rintala, Diana H. "Predictive Validity of Social Support Relative to Psychological Well-Being in Men with Spinal Cord Injury." *Rehabilitation Psychology* 58 (2013) 422–28.
Robeck, Cecil M., Jr. "Montanism and Present Day 'Prophets.'" *Pneuma* 32 (2010) 413–29.
Roberts, Brent W., and Daniel Mroczek. "Personality Trait Change in Adulthood." *Current Directions in Psychological Science* 17 (2008) 31–35.
Robertson, Brian J., and Tom Thomison. "Holacracy: The New Management System for a Rapidly Changing World." HolacracyOne, LLC. http://www.holacracy.org.
Robins, Clive J., Shian-Ling Keng, Andrew G. Ekblad and Jeffrey G. Brantley. "Effects of Mindfulness-Based Stress Reduction on Emotional Experience and Expression: A Randomized Controlled Trial." *Journal of Clinical Psychology* 68 (2012) 117–31.
Roeser, Robert W., and Jacquelynne S. Eccles. "Mindfulness and Compassion in Human Development: Introduction to the Special Section." *Developmental Psychology* 51 (2015) 1–6.
Rohr, Richard. "True Prayer Leads to Compassion." Richard Rohr's Daily Meditation. July 2, 2014. http://myemail.constantcontact.com/Richard-Rohr-s-Meditation—True-Prayer-Leads-to-Compassion.html?soid=1103098668616&aid=yjngM7jJVDg.
Rosaldo, Michelle Z. "Moral-Analytic Dilemmas Posed by the Intersection of Feminism and Social Science." In Norma Haan, *Social Science as Moral Inquiry*, 76–95. New York: Columbia University Press, 1983.
Rosenzweig, Franz. *The Star of Redemption*. Boston: Beacon, 1972.
Rublev, Andrei. *The Trinity* (1411 or 1427–27). https://en.wikipedia.org/wiki/Trinity_(Andrei_Rublev)

Bibliography

Ryan, Richard M., and Kirk Warren Brown. "Why We Don't Need Self-Esteem: On Fundamental Needs, Contingent Love, and Mindfulness." *Psychological Inquiry* 14 (2003) 71–76.
Sáez, Ignacio, Lusha Zhu, Eric Set, Andrew Kayser, and Ming Hsu. "Dopamine Modulates Egalitarian Behavior in Humans." *Current Biology* 25 (2015) 912–19.
Salzman, Philip Carl. "Is Inequality Universal?" *Current Anthropology* 40 (1999) 31–44.
Sanchez, Roxanne, Jeffrey C. Parkin, Jennie Y. Chen, and Peter B. Gray. "Oxytocin, Vasopressin, and Human Social Behavior." In *Endocrinology of Social Relationships*, edited by Peter T. Ellison and Peter B. Gray, 319–39. Cambridge, MA: Harvard University Press, 2009.
Schaller, Mark. *Evolution, Culture, and the Human Mind*. New York: Psychology, 2010.
Schertzer, Susan M. B., Daniel Laufer, David H. Silvera, and J. Brad McBride. "A Cross-Cultural Validation of a Gender Role Identity Scale in Marketing." *International Marketing Review* 25 (2008) 312–23.
Scholl, Annika and Kai Sassenberg. "'While You Still Think, I Already Type': Experienced Social Power Reduces Deliberation During E-Mail Communication." *CyberPsychology, Behavior & Social Networking* 17 (2014) 692–96.
Shonin, Edo. "This Is Not Mcmindfulness by Any Stretch of the Imagination." *The Psychologist* (2015). http://thepsychologist.bps.org.uk/not-mcmindfulness-any-stretch-imagination.
Shoul, Mark, and Philip W. Rabinowitz. "Building Hope in a De-industrializing Community: Creating a New Kind of Community Organization to Mobilize the Politically Sidelined Majority around the Issue of Building Civic Cultures of Collaboration." *National Civic Review* 100 (2011) 36–47.
Singer, Tania, Romana Snozzi, Geoffrey Bird, Predrag Petrovic, Giorgia Silani, Markus Heinrichs, and Raymond J. Dolan. "Effects of Oxytocin and Prosocial Behavior on Brain Responses to Direct and Vicariously Experienced Pain." *Emotion* 8 (2008) 781–91.
Snodgrass, Klyne. "Paul's Focus on Identity." *Bibliotheca sacra* 168 (2011) 259–73.
Snyder, Howard A. *The Problem of Wineskins: Church Structure in a Technological Age*. Downers Grove, IL: InterVarsity, 1975.
Snyder, Nicole S. Oliver. "The Impact of Mindfulness Practice and Group Leadership Training on Identification with Stereotypic Sex Role Attributes in Christian Leadership Groups." DMin thesis, Denver Seminary, 2016.
Spong, Martha, ed. *There's a Woman in the Pulpit: Christian Clergywomen Share Their Hard Days, Holy Moments and the Healing Power of Humor*. Woodstock, VT: SkyLight Paths Publishing, 2012.
Stark, Rodney. *The Rise of Christianity: How the Obscure, Marginal Jesus Movement Became the Dominant Religious Force in the Western World in a Few Centuries*. San Francisco: HarperSanFrancisco, 1997.
Steinbeis, Nikolaus, and Tania Singer. "Projecting My Envy onto You: Neurocognitive Mechanisms of an Offline Emotional Egocentricity Bias." *NeuroImage* 102 (2014) 370–80.
"Sticky Faith." (2012). http://stickyfaith.org/about-sticky-faith.
Strang, Veronica. "Lording It over the Goddess." *Journal of Feminist Studies in Religion* 30 (2014) 85–109.

Bibliography

Stuart, Elizabeth. "Turning Towards the Tomb: Priesthood and Gender." *Theology & Sexuality: The Journal of the Institute for the Study of Christianity & Sexuality* 10 (2003) 30–39.

Su, Yuling, Rong-Ji Pan, and Kun-Hu Chen. "Encountering Selves and Others: Finding Meaning in Life through Action and Reflection on a Social Service Learning Program." *Journal of Pacific Rim Psychology* 8 (2014) 43–52.

Tanay, Galia, and Amit Bernstein. "State Mindfulness Scale (SMS): Development and Initial Validation." *Psychological Assessment* 25 (2013) 1286–99.

Thiselton, Anthony C. "The Significance of Recent Research on 1 Corinthians for Hermeneutical Appropriation of This Epistle Today." *Neotestamentica* 40 (2006) 320–52.

Tinker, George E. *Spirit and Resistance: Political Theology and American Indian Liberation*. Minneapolis: Fortress, 2004.

Tippett, Krista. *OnBeing: The Big Questions of Meaning* (2016) http://www.onbeing.org/

Towner, W. Sibley. "Clones of God: Genesis 1:26–28 and the Image of God in the Hebrew Bible." *Interpretation* 59 (2005) 341–56.

Tran, Mai-Anh Le. "Narrating Lives, Narrating Faith: 'Organic Hybridity' for Contemporary Christian Religious Education." *Religious Education* 105 (2010) 188–203.

Tsukamoto, Saori, Elise Holland, Nick Haslam, Minoru Karasawa, and Yoshihisa Kashima. "Cultural Differences in Perceived Coherence of the Self and Ingroup: A Japan-Australia Comparison." *Asian Journal of Social Psychology* 18 (2015) 83–89.

Turner, Denys. "'Sin Is Behovely' in Julian of Norwich's Revelations of Divine Love." *Modern Theology* 20 (2004) 407–22.

Verhofstadt, Lesley L., and Fanny Weytens. "Biological Sex and Gender Role Identity as Predictors of Spousal Support Provision: A Scenario-Based Study." *Journal of Gender Studies* 22 (2013) 166–77.

Vest, Norvene. "Is Reverie to Be Trusted? The Imaginal and the Work of Marija Gimbutas." *Feminist Theology: The Journal of the Britain & Ireland School of Feminist Theology* 13 (2005) 239–48.

Vogels, Walter. "'It Is Not Good That the "Mensch" Should Be Alone; I Will Make Him/Her a Helper Fit for Him/Her' (Gen 2:18)." *Eglise et Théologie* 9 (1978) 9–35.

von Humboldt, Wilhelm. *Über die Verschiedenheiten des menschlichen Sprachbaues (1827–29), Werke III* (Schriften zur Sprachphilosophie) ed, A. Flitner and K. Giel, 191.

Walden, Wayne. "Galatians 3:28: Grammar Observations." *Restoration Quarterly* 51 (2009) 45–50.

Waltke, Bruce K., and Cathi J. Fredricks. *Genesis: A Commentary*. Grand Rapids, MI: Zondervan, 2001.

Warren Brown, Kirk, and Richard M. Ryan. "Why We Don't Need Self-Esteem: On Fundamental Needs, Contingent Love, and Mindfulness." *Psychological Inquiry* 14 (2003) 55.

Warren Brown, Kirk, and Tim Kasser. "Are Psychological and Ecological Well-Being Compatible? The Role of Values, Mindfulness, and Lifestyle." *Social Indicators Research* 74 (2005) 349–68.

Watson, Wilfred G. E. *Classical Hebrew Poetry: A Guide to Its Techniques* T&T Clark Biblical Languages. New York: T&T Clark, 2005.

Bibliography

Weinstein, Netta, William S. Ryan, Cody R. DeHaan, Andrew K. Przybylski, Nicole Legate, and Richard M. Ryan. "Parental Autonomy Support and Discrepancies between Implicit and Explicit Sexual Identities: Dynamics of Self-Acceptance and Defense." *Journal of Personality and Social Psychology* 102 (2012) 815–32.

Welz, Claudia. "Imago Dei: References to the Invisible." *Studia theologica* 65 (2011) 74–91.

Wesley Hymn Collection." Northwest Nazarene University (2015). http://wesley.nnu.edu/charles-wesley/wesley-hymn-collection.

Wheatley, Margaret J. "Self-Organized Networks." *Leadership Excellence* 25 (2008) 7.

Wheeless, Virginia E., and Paul F. Potorti. "Student Assessment of Teacher Masculinity and Femininity: A Test of the Sex Role Congruency Hypothesis on Student Attitudes toward Learning." *Journal of Educational Psychology* 81 (1989) 259–62.

Williams, J. Mark G., and Jon Kabat-Zinn. "Mindfulness: Diverse Perspectives on Its Meaning, Origins, and Multiple Applications at the Intersection of Science and Dharma." *Contemporary Buddhism* 12 (2011) 1–18.

Wilson, Timothy D., David A. Reinhard, Erin C. Westgate, Daniel T. Gilbert, Nicole Ellerbeck, Cheryl Hahn, Casey L. Brown, and Adi Shaked. "Just Think: The Challenges of the Disengaged Mind." *Science* 345 (2014) 75–77.

Witkiewitz, Katie, and Sarah Bowen. "Depression, Craving, and Substance Use Following a Randomized Trial of Mindfulness-Based Relapse Prevention." *Journal of Consulting and Clinical Psychology* 78 (2010) 362–74.

Witkiewitz, Katie, Sarah Bowen, Haley Douglas, and Sharon H. Hsu. "Mindfulness-Based Relapse Prevention for Substance Craving." *Addictive Behaviors* 38 (2013) 1563–71.

Wong, Paul T. P. "Meaning Therapy: Assessments and Interventions." *Existential Analysis: Journal of the Society for Existential Analysis* 26 (2015) 154–67.

Wongpakaran, Tinakon, Nahathai Wongpakaran, Rojarek Intachote-Sakamoto, and Theerarat Boripuntakul. "The Group Cohesiveness Scale (GCS) for Psychiatric Inpatients." *Perspectives in Psychiatric Care* 49 (2013) 58–64.

Wood, Wendy, and Alice H. Eagly. "A Cross-Cultural Analysis of the Behavior of Women and Men: Implications for the Origins of Sex Differences." *Psychological Bulletin* 128 (2002) 699–727.

Yildirim, Caglar, and Ana-Paula Correia. "Exploring the Dimensions of Nomophobia: Development and Validation of a Self-Reported Questionnaire." *Computers in Human Behavior* 49 (2015) 130–37.

Zagefka, Hanna, and Limabenla Jamir. "Conflict, Fear and Social Identity in Nagaland." *Asian Journal of Social Psychology* 18 (2015) 43–51.

Ziefle, Helmut W. *Modern Theological German: A Reader and Dictionary*. Grand Rapids, MI: Baker Books, 1997.

Zizioulas, John D. *Being as Communion*. Crestwood, NY: St. Vladimir's Seminary Press, 1985.

www.ingramcontent.com/pod-product-compliance
Lightning Source LLC
Chambersburg PA
CBHW051938160426
43198CB00013B/2210